# A History of Immigrant Roman Catholics and Converts in Early Singapore 1832–1945

(2nd Edition)

*by*

**Marc Sebastian Rerceretnam**

All rights reserved. No part of this publication may be reproduced or transmitted in any form or by any means, without prior permission in writing from the author/publisher.

Correspondence should be directed to: Dr Marc Sebastian Rerceretnam, 272 Holden Street, Ashbury NSW 2193, Australia or marc@hwy.com.au

Copyright © 2021 Marc Sebastian Rerceretnam
*All rights reserved*

For available supplementary material, please visit
Facebook: The History of the Roman Catholic Church in Singapore
Website: https://tansofmakepeaceroad.wordpress.com/

Every effort has been made to trace copyright holders and to obtain their permission for use of copyright material. The publisher apologises for any errors or omissions and is happy to rectify them in any future reprints, if notified of them.

First edition published by Marc Sebastian Rerceretnam PhD, Singapore/Australia 2021
Second edition published by Marc Sebastian Rerceretnam PhD, Singapore/Australia 2023
marc@hwy.com.au

ISBN: 978-0-6452364-0-8

Printed in Singapore
Design by Janice Cheong, Gerakbudaya, Malaysia

Editor: Ilsa Sharp Editorial Services, Perth W. Australia
sharpeditor@iinet.net.au

This book is dedicated to
My mother Phyllis, my aunts Marjorie, Janice, Doreen, Emmeline, Clarice, uncles Vincent and Francis, and my grandparents Cecilia and Philip.

'We chose the camaraderie of this faith, we do not fear you.
When we return to China, we will be Christians.
And if we are killed, we will go to heaven.
As for the pigtail, and our Chinese clothes,
you can take them off and you can cut our heads and tear our skin.
By harming us, you make us happy'.

Source: Annals of the Propagation of the Faith, XLII, 10 September. 1833.

Declaration made by one of the following Teochew Chinese men, converted on 18 August 1833, in defiance of the hostile Singapore Teochew Kongsi: Francis Ah Fa (aged 35), Francis Ah Li (36), Joseph Ah Hee (29) or Vincent Ah Kiau (31).

Front cover picture

*Photo of 21-year-old Mathilda Chia (1896–1985), in traditional Melaka-style Nyonya wedding dress on her marriage to 23-year-old, Bangkok-based Joseph Low Kwang Seng at Saints Peter & Paul's Church, 25 June 1917.*
Source: Mr Prrida Komolkiti, Bangkok.

# Contents

| | |
|---|---|
| *Preface* by Vicar General/Chancellor, The Roman Catholic Archdiocese of Singapore | vii |
| *Foreword* by Peter Lee | ix |
| *Acknowledgements* | xi |

| | |
|---|---|
| **Chapter 1. Setting the Scene** | 1 |
| Arrival of Christianity | 2 |
| From Home to Singapore | 3 |
| Arrivals from Guangdong Province, China | 3 |
| The Melaka Portuguese and Eurasians | 8 |
| India and Ceylon | 10 |
| The French, English, Irish and other Europeans | 13 |
| | |
| **Chapter 2. The Multiracial Landscape of Early Singapore** | 17 |
| Establishment of the Roman Catholic church | 18 |
| Conversion – the Chinese community | 20 |
| Conversion – Melaka Portuguese, Eurasians and Malays | 25 |
| Conversion – South Asian community | 27 |
| Strategic omissions and the adoption of new names | 30 |
| Intermarriage within the Catholic church | 34 |
| Singapore's first homegrown Peranakan bloodline | 38 |
| The Life of Pedro Tan Nong Keah (1808–c.1886) | 40 |
| | |
| **Chapter 3. Clans and *Kongsi*** | 53 |
| Teochew clan conflict with the Catholics | 54 |
| The Anti-Catholic Riots of 1851 | 56 |
| | |
| **Chapter 4. Growth of Roman Catholic Businesses and Patronage** | 63 |
| The Church needs cash | 64 |
| Farmers | 65 |
| The 1892 Saints Peter & Paul's Church benefactors' marble tablet | 66 |

The Ellenborough 'New Market', Clarke Quay  69
The philanthropic first wave, 1840–1880: Pedro Tan Nong Keah  71
The philanthropic second wave, 1880s–1930: Small and
large businesses emerge  72
The philanthropic third wave, 1930–1945: Grassroots organising,
more businesses arise  81

## Chapter 5. The Role of Women, Marriage and Matchmaking  95
Women  96
The different roles of women  98
Marriage  101
Homosexuality  103
Female orphans, and males desperately seeking respectability  104
Orphanages  107
Intermarriages  111
Intra-ethnic divisions  115
Social conservatism and divisions  118
Gender interaction  119
Interaction between priests and parishioners  120
Matchmakers and marriages between family groups  121
Marriage during the Japanese Occupation  129

## Chapter 6. Catholic Education Fills the Colonial Gap  135
The founding of Catholic schools  137
St Joseph's Institution  139
The Convent of the Holy Infant Jesus  141
The key role played by Catholic schools  144
Colonials keeping 'natives' in their place  145

## Chapter 7. The Roman Catholic Church: Architect of Multiracial Education & Social Services in Colonial Singapore  149
Multiracialism  150
Education  151
Social services  151

# Preface

By its very name which means 'universal', the Catholic Church is a melting pot of many races, cultures, languages, social classes, and educational backgrounds. This is true both in colonial and modern-day Singapore. United by one faith, we learnt to navigate the complex web of interactions with our neighbours and friends. Today, it is essential for the Church to continue to draw from the lessons of the past, even as we move forward as Church, since our identity is rooted in the contributions of those who came before us and the challenges they faced.

*The Church and its Converts* gives us a glimpse into the lives of our forebears. Dr Rerceretnam tells the story of how the colonial Church bridged diverse backgrounds in schools, parishes, and in providing social services to the wider community. He notes the ways in which the Church provided for the social and educational needs of non-Europeans in early Singapore, and how this benefited subsequent generations. His research covers multiple issues of colonial Singaporean social history from Catholic perspectives and sources and does not shy away from the imperfections of the Church in its attempts to organise itself in the early decades.

This book is illustrated with stories from ordinary lay people who recount how their ancestors (and they themselves) understood the growing Church. Such memories are important to our history and consequently, our identity. Dr Rerceretnam has written an interesting work that adds to the existing narrative on Singapore and the Church.

It is my wish that this work, and others like it, may spark a greater interest in local Church history and inspire others to keep the stories of our Catholic families and communities alive for generations to come.

**Rev. Msgr John Paul Tan OFM, JCL**
Vicar General / Chancellor
The Roman Catholic Archdiocese of Singapore, 2021

# Foreword

It is not often that a history of Singapore can be told from the elusive intersections between the worlds of the colonial state, religion and the local people. Government reference sources, rare church records, family documents and personal recollections come together to unveil a unique, untold narrative of the nation's past. Dr Marc Rerceretnam's work achieves this while drawing our perspective of Singapore's history away from the traditional colonial lens, towards a more balanced (and what I also believe to be, a decolonial) viewpoint. How we constantly re-evaluate the past reshapes how we understand ourselves.

As someone who pays close attention to the evolution of hybrid cultures in the region, I am particularly excited by the way Marc reveals the Catholic church's position as an important nexus of hybrid cultures and mixed marriages in Singapore. The history of the Catholic church in Asia is intertwined with that of colonialisation. The church has from its beginnings in Goa in the early sixteenth century, been a very important conduit for one of colonialisation's by-products — hybrid cultures, mixed marriages and multiracial communities. How well these have sustained over the centuries! I have known Marc since we were both in Primary 1 at St Michael's School, a Catholic institution, over fifty years ago. Our class was an exuberant mix of Eurasian, Indian, European, Filipino and Chinese boys. Growing up in this plural and Catholic milieu in multiracial Singapore conditioned us to investigate histories of interconnections.

My research has primarily focused on widening the spectrum of Peranakan identity. There is nothing homogenous about being Peranakan. And there is nothing romantic about the idea of the Peranakan either. The histories of port cities and of diverse communities coming together have always been about volatility, disorder, racism and elitism, as much as about multiculturalism, hybrid art, civic consciousness and philanthropy. Peranakan and Singapore history mirror the full gamut of these qualities, summed up in the title of the equally hybrid spaghetti western classic, *The Good, the Bad and the Ugly*. In every sense of the word, no-one, no culture, no community, is pure. Marc's fascinating narratives about the evolution of the Malacca Eurasians and Teochew Christian Peranakans in Singapore not only reinforce the notion that Peranakan families and communities formed in diverse ways, but that the process was fraught with social injustice, and not a few scandals as well. The only way to transcend colonial versions of history and to present authentic decolonialised history, is to look, not through a glass darkly but face to face, at the good, the bad and the ugly, on *all* sides.

**Peter Lee**
Independent Scholar

# Acknowledgements

When I started my research journey back in 1996, it was essentially an exercise of filling in the blanks in my family history. Little more than a decade later, I began to realise my family's experience was part of a much larger and more remarkable story. This book is a culmination of this ongoing project.

There are many people I would like to thank for helping with this book. Firstly, I would like to thank my wife Merete and my three daughters for putting up with me. A great outcome of all this research has been the reuniting of my extended maternal family. Over the decades, the many branches have lost touch or never even met. A mutual interest in our family history joined us all, and was aided by social media. This newfound group has been a huge source of support, socially and occasionally, financially. From this group, I found a fellow researcher and collaborator, Juliana Lim - my partner in crime! We both share a keen interest in local history and egged and encouraged each other on throughout the research and writing process.

This project is also a direct offshoot of research done as part of a 2019 Lee Kong Chian research fellowship. That short six-month stint provided me with a window to explore new networks, make new friends and cherish new experiences. I would like to thank the National Library Board's Tan Huism, Joanna Tan and Lee Meiyu. Extensive support was also provided by the Roman Catholic Archdiocese of Singapore. In this endeavour (Chancellor) Fr John Paul Tan OFM, Jennifer Joseph, St Joseph's Institution's Fr Adrian Danker, Nervina D'Rozario and Andrew Koh and CHIJ's Sr Daniel Ee (Kuala Lumpur) and Sr Maria Lau (Singapore), were indispensable. They arranged and facilitated essential access to key archival documents, which made this book possible.

During my research, I was introduced to many community organisations and inspiring individuals. The Peranakan Association of Singapore (TPAS) takes pride of place here. My many discussions with TPAS stalwarts Colin Chee, Peter Lee and Tan Koon Siang, and later with

Ponnusamy Kalastree from their Indian counterpart (Peranakan Indian Association Singapore) helped me conceptualise my study within a much larger and older multi-ethnic and culturally hybrid landscape. Also, a special thank you goes out to Julia d'Silva and Jacqueline Perris from the Eurasian Association, Singapore, and my friend Vernon Adrian Emuang, founder of *Serani Sembang*. I am also eager to acknowledge a new circle of local authors and historians, such as Shawn Seah, Cyprian Lim, Peter Lee and Juliana Lim, who critiqued, advised and answered my many questions. I would also like to acknowledge research assistance work by Khoo Ee Hoon in the early stages of the project (2016-2017).

I would also like to express gratitude for key financial support from the following persons. They helped get this self-published venture off the ground; Lucille Lam, Songak Tobsbowon, Caroline Lim, John Tay Loy Sek, Marcella, Jan, Mike and Martin van der Klooster, and finally the Wee siblings ; Marjorie van der Klooster (late); Francis Wee (late); Janice Lui; Vincent Wee; Phyllis Sebastian; Doreen Ruangsangwatana; Emmeline le Meilleur (late), and Clarice Wee-Thng.

**Marc Sebastian Rerceretnam Ph.D.**
1 July 2021

Chapter 1

# Setting the Scene

Singapore has a history going back to at least the thirteenth century of the Christian era. However, by the time the British arrived there in the late 1700s, the island had seen better days, and had reverted to a sleepy regional trading backwater.

When British East India Company officials Stamford Raffles and William Farquhar arrived in Singapore in February 1819, the dominant inhabitants of the island were various Malayo-Indonesian communities who were mainly fishermen, boatmen and farmers. These included the Bugis seafarers who commanded shipping and trade routes between Singapore and their homeland in the Celebes region (today's Sulawesi region of Indonesia). They shipped in a variety of spices, coffee, and gold dust. According to Singaporean historians Kwa and Kua (*A General History of the Chinese in Singapore*) there were approximately thirty Chinese living on the island. Immigrants from the Teochew and Hokkien language groups of southern China were well established in the neighbouring Riau islands, and in Indonesia and Melaka (Malacca, in the southern part of today's peninsular Malaysia). Many ran profitable gambier plantations in the region, growing the valuable gambier vine, popular as an additive to the stimulant betel-nut chewing 'tobacco', and as an important tanning and dyeing agent.[1]

After the British established themselves on Singapore island in 1819, it immediately became a primary destination for Teochew migrants with wealthy trading families flocking to this new British free port.[2] Tan Che Seng, Choa Chong Long and Seah Eu Chin were examples of early well-to-do business entrepreneurs who settled in Singapore.[3] By 1821, the population of the island was estimated at 4,727 persons, including

2,851 Malays, 1,159 Chinese and 29 Europeans. The following year, South Indians began arriving. However, within only a few more years, many Chinese immigrants started arriving from various parts of the southern Guangdong province of China, becoming the largest group in Singapore. There were also some 'Peranakan' Chinese – whose Malayan roots and hybridised culture dating back several centuries – arriving from around the region, largely employed as brokers, shopkeepers and general merchants. The newer Chinese arrivals, at this stage mostly Teochews, were more involved in local industry.

## Arrival of Christianity

Of the major foreign belief systems that proliferated in the Malay Archipelago, Hinduism and Islam initially were paramount. Both Buddhism and Hinduism made an early appearance in the periods of the seventh to eleventh (Srivijaya Empire) and the thirteenth to sixteenth centuries (Majapahit Empire) respectively. Hinduism also spread as a result of contact with Hindu Indian traders from South Indian ports. Hindu Brahmin priests reportedly converted tribal chiefs to Hinduism and according to Chinese sources, even intermarried into local families.

Islam was the next major religious influence and would later supplant Hinduism. Reports by Chinese chroniclers of the presence of Islam date back to as early as 622. However, Islam probably did not gain a strong foothold till the arrival of Arab, Persian and Indian merchants.

Christianity arrived in the Malay Archipelago with the Portuguese invasion of Melaka in 1511. However, the religion they brought with them had little long-term effect on local populations in the region. Consequently, it remained only within the limited confines of a small community of mixed Melakan Portuguese 'Kristang'-speaking (Portuguese dialect) descendants in Melaka. It took several centuries before a new wave of Christian evangelisation became apparent with the arrival of British interests, and then generally with more recent non-Muslim immigrant arrivals. In 1781, with the help of the Sultan of Kedah, French Roman Catholic missionaries set up a station in Kedah, where they oversaw a group of Catholic refugees from Siam.[4] Following the British occupation of Penang island in 1786, this parish moved to the new island outpost. By the early nineteenth century, the Roman Catholic church was the largest Christian denomination in the Malay Archipelago.[5] Following the establishment of the British on the island of Singapore in February 1819, French priest Reverend Imbert visited Singapore in 1822 and reported to the Bishop of Siam that the island had twelve or thirteen Catholics who lived a 'wretched' life.[6] By 1832, French missionaries had formed a permanent base in Singapore, led by Reverend Jean-Baptiste Boucho (later Bishop) and Padre Anselmo Yegros,[7] when the British colonial government granted them rent-free land on Bras Basah Road for the purposes of worship.

## From Home to Singapore

By 1821, there were more than 5,000 people living on the island and Teochews made up a large proportion of the Chinese community. Up to this point, locally settled Bugis had dominated shipping and trade between Singapore and the Celebes region, but their dominance of the local communities and the island's economy was soon challenged by continuous waves of Teochew, and later Hokkien-speaking migrants, from the coastal towns of China. They were joined to a lesser extent by regionally domiciled Chinese from the surrounding region.[8] By the late 1820s, these new migrants outnumbered the indigenous communities (Orang Asli aboriginals, semi-itinerant Orang Laut or 'sea gypsies', and an often-shifting Malayo-Indonesian group) on the island. It is extremely difficult to identify precisely all the myriad villages and regions of China from which Catholic migrants originated. What this research has attempted to do is identify and place the main migration sources.

## Arrivals from Guangdong Province, China

Leaving your family, friends and social networks is never an easy process. Such decisions are usually made under duress, a drastic, forced reaction to poverty and thwarted aspirations when few other opportunities or choices exist. The early church mainly comprised three groups: the

Teochews and a much smaller number of Hakkas from the northern region of Guangdong province, Melakan Portuguese who migrated to Singapore from around June 1819, and South Indians from India and Ceylon (Sri Lanka) – and smaller batches of Eurasians and Europeans.

The earliest Chinese parishioners at the original Bras Basah Road chapel, in the 1830s, were Teochew-speakers from the Shantou (Swatow) region, located in the northern region of Guangdong province. Christianity made its way into China via European imperialism and ensuing missionary activity. Religious communities sprang up in various parts of China, especially among port or coastal communities where contact with new European influences was common. The coastal city of Shantou was one of these places. The French organisation, Missions Étrangères de Paris (the Foreign Missions of Paris [MEP]), had already

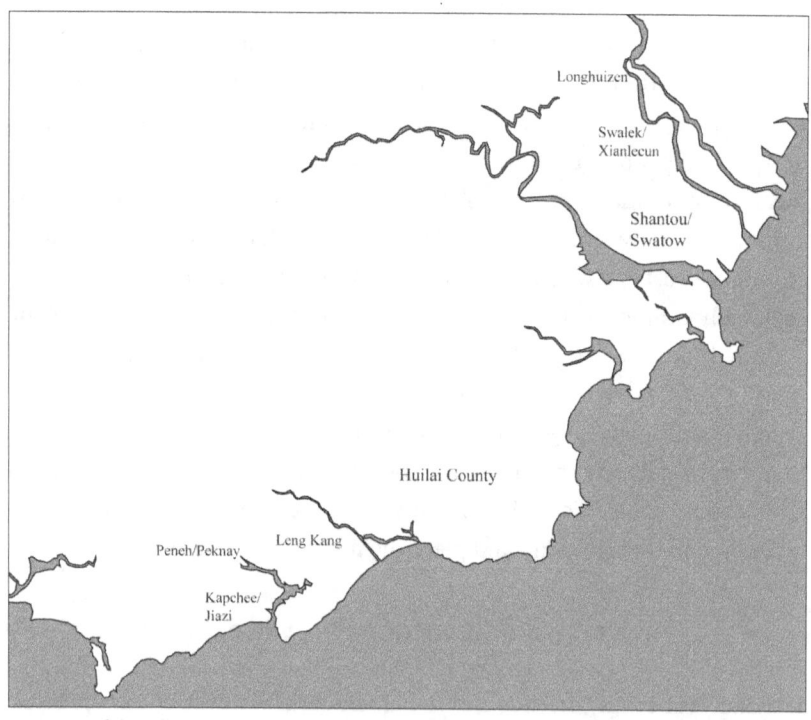

*Some of the villages in the Shantou/Swatow and Huilai region where Catholic Teochew families originate.*

Source: Cyprian Lim and author.

established themselves in the Shantou area by the late Ming dynasty period, around the early 1600s. They were in what is today known as Huilai county (惠来). By the nineteenth century, European Roman Catholic missionaries, primarily led by French MEP members, were established in Shantou county, along with other rival Protestant missions.

Both the Teochew-speaking Shantou and Huilai counties played a disproportionately large role in the supply of Catholic parishioners to Singapore in the first few decades after the formation of the Catholic mission on Bras Basah Road in 1832. While many were converted in Singapore, there is a strong possibility that many more arrivals were already Catholic on arrival in Singapore. The village of Peknay or Peneh (百冷乡) is a case in point: its Catholic community dates to the 1600s, although the village itself was relocated to its present site in the 1700s. Other Huilai county (惠来) villages have been identified as possible sources, such as Kapchee (甲子) also known as Jiazi, Chia-tzu, Jiazi Zhen and Kapchi. Another was Leng Kang (隆江), also known as Longjiang. At the time of writing (2020) only brief information on two Teochew

*Peknay/Peneh (百冷乡) Catholic Church, located in Teochew-speaking Huilai county*

Source: Cyprian Lim

Catholic villages exists. Peknay/Peneh (百冷乡) village or Bailingcun (白冷村), has been covered extensively by Singaporean historian Cyprian Lim in his 2019 book *My Maternal Roots*. Lim records how this village contained various Teochew families, bearing the names Koh (Xu 許), Lee (Li 李), Teo (Zhang 張), Boon (Wen 文) and Lim (Lin 林).

While the main cluster of early Catholic villages resided in Huilai county, several more also existed about ten to twenty kilometres east, in Shantou county. Also worthy of mention are the Hakka-speaking converts who made up a small part of this early congregation. The Hakka-speaking region is located immediately south of the Teochew areas. Among the villages these Hakkas originated from are Hai Lok Fong (海陆丰), a Catholic Hakka village located west of Huilai county in Shanwei city, and villages in the Jiaoling county in Meizhou area (鎮平縣招福鄉). There is evidence that some of these Hakkas intermarried with Teochew parishioners in Singapore during the 1830s and 1840s.

*The tombstone of Goh Siong Jin (1817– 1858), a Hakka, St Joseph's Church cemetery, Bukit Timah, Singapore, 2019*

*Source: Author*

In the city of Shantou, a predominantly Catholic village called Swalek (仙乐) or Xianlecun (仙乐村) exists to this day. It was not converted as early as some of the Huilai villages. Most of its Catholic adherents' ancestors adopted the new faith in Singapore from (probably) the early 1860s. Swalek appears to be dominated by Teochew families holding the Low (盧) clan name or surname. A church was built in 1901. Funds for the construction of Swalek's Holy Rosary Church came from Singapore and Bangkok-based Low family members. The church was named in commemoration of another church with the same name in Bangkok which had been consecrated several years earlier in 1897 and was also heavily funded by the same Low family members.

*Mass celebrated by the Bishop of Shantou at the Holy Rosary Church, Swalek (仙乐)*
*2 December 2019*

Source: Author

Another Catholic church, located in the Longhuizen (龙湖镇) area in Shantou city, is the Church of the Blessed Virgin. The church was established in 1905 and is only a few kilometres north of Swalek (仙乐).

More villages have been identified but further research is still needed to identify how prevalent Catholicism was within these localities. Villages like Dai Jingguan (戴金冠), Dai Deguan (戴德冠), Dai Wulüe (戴勿略, Xavier Dai), Shimen (石门), are all located in the Huilai area. Other villages are Shukeng (书坑) in Jiayingzhou, Shangdong (上洞), Yunluo (云落) town in Puning (普宁) district, Donghu (东湖) village, Lingting (岭亭) village, Wucuo (吴厝) village in West Gate and Chenghai (澄海) villages.[9]

## The Melaka Portuguese and Eurasians

When the Catholic church in Singapore was consecrated in May 1833, the Melaka Portuguese community made up around 90% of its early congregation. Back in 1819, Lt Colonel Farquhar had publicised new and better opportunities in Singapore and this news had reached places like Melaka.[10] It is highly probably that large numbers from the Melaka Portuguese community took advantage of this opportunity, alongside their fellow Malay, Chinese and Indian Melakans. By the early 1830s, it was reported there were approximately 300 Catholic parishioners in Singapore, and judging from entries in early church registers, the Melaka Portuguese community did dominate the congregation at the time. Although a Melaka Portuguese-specific mission had existed on the island since 1825, the Portuguese Mission had done little to establish itself properly. In contrast, the rapid growth of the new French-based mission at this time, suggests that the Catholic community preferred the new French-run chapel on Bras Basah Road.

The Melaka Portuguese community was a diverse community from Melaka town, located about 200 kilometres north of Singapore, located at the southern end of the Malayan peninsula. The town of Melaka was founded in the early 1400s by a hereditary Malay Sultanate and became a bustling maritime trading centre within a few decades. However, by 1509, Portugal became aware of the town's strategic position overlooking the Melaka Strait shipping route, running parallel to the neighbouring major Indonesian island of Sumatra, and of its key role in the spice trade; in 1511 Portugal duly invaded Melaka and removed the Sultanate, holding the town till 1641, when the Dutch seized it after a long siege. In turn, the Dutch ruled Melaka until 1824, when they agreed do a swap with the British, exchanging Melaka for Batavia (now Jakarta). This move helped the two colonial powers consolidate their respective colonial possessions in the Malay Archipelago (British) and present-day Indonesia (Dutch).

The 'Portuguese' label adopted by a section of the Melaka community belies its diverse heritage. The tag is based on the assertion that these are the offspring of local Malay females consorting with the Portuguese males who held Melaka for just over a century. However, historical evidence says otherwise, and even shows a considerable Indian and even African composition within the Portuguese occupation force. There is also debate on how the concept of race, or the Portuguese label, probably did not hold that strong a place in early identity. That is probably why terms such as 'Serani' still persist to this day. The term 'Serani' is probably a local variation of 'Nazarani' or a person adhering to a faith associated with 'Nazareth', which denotes one's faith rather than one's racial grouping. Like the rest of mixed Melakan society, there already existed a diverse Peranakan heritage within the existing Hokkien, Chetti and Jawi communities. They probably saw themselves as a Christian version of those communities.[11]

After Portugal's departure in 1641, new admixtures with Dutch, English or Irish bloodlines were introduced into the blend. In the nineteenth and twentieth centuries, the Melaka community was divided into two distinct social classes defined by wealth, education, and occupation. The upper class, known as the 'Upper Tens' preferred to identify themselves with the new colonial British category 'Eurasian'. These people tended to have Dutch or British surnames, although a minority did possess Portuguese names too. They were literate, spoke English at home and usually held white-collar jobs at British firms. On the other hand, the 'Portuguese' (also referred to as the 'Lower Sixes')[12] were mainly illiterate, spoke the local Portuguese creole called 'Kristang', and mostly worked as fishmongers and fishermen. While the majority had Portuguese surnames, a good number of this group bore Dutch and British family names. Some of the early Melaka Portuguese families in Singapore were named Fernandez, Pereira, Sequeira, Lazaroo, Da Costa, Gomes, Panna, Pedro, Rodrigues, Rozells, Monteiro and de Rosario.

This Melaka Portuguese group dominated the early Singapore Catholic church till the middle to late 1840s. After this point, their numerical dominance was surpassed by newly arrived Teochew converts to the faith. By 1853, many Melaka Portuguese had left the French Mission churches for the newly built Portuguese Mission-controlled St Joseph's Church, located a few hundred metres away, on Victoria Street. The ones that remained were largely 'Upper Tens'. Some Teochews who married Melaka Portuguese women did follow their wives to this new church too.

Apart from the Melakan 'Upper Tens', new groups of Eurasians from the region joined the congregation. They were primarily from Penang, Bencoolen (now Bengkulu city, Sumatra) and Indian cities like Madras (Chennai, Tamil Nadu). They were usually products of English, Irish or European relationships with local women. They appeared to mix mostly with each other, although over time, they did socially mix and intermarry with the local Melakan 'Upper Tens'. The most prominent Melakan 'Upper Ten' was J. I. Woodford. He acted as the general church catechist for many years and ran a pharmacy in Singapore.

## India and Ceylon

Most South Asian migrants to Singapore came from India and Ceylon. Christianity in India can be traced to the first century of the Christian era. The present-day Syrian Christian Church of Travancore believe their branch of Christianity was founded by St Thomas himself in the first century – 'Doubting Thomas' was one of the twelve biblical apostles of Jesus Christ. According to the Syrian Christian story, Thomas arrived in Year 52 of the Christian era, to preach to the Jews of Malabar, but in time began preaching to other locals as well. From this came India's first indigenous Christian community, and the forerunners of the present-day Syrian Christian community in India's south-western Kerala state.[13] The 'Syrians' are also well represented in the Singapore of today. Other independent accounts from the third century tell of an episode where Vellalar-caste (farmer/landowners) Christian families escaping persecution joined a Syrian Christian church in Malabar. Another account, probably of the same incident, tells of seventy-two Vellalar families fleeing from the imperial Tamil Chola dynasty's persecution in Puhar and seeking refuge in Quilon.[14] Christian influences in the Indian subcontinent remained primarily marginal despite the region's early exposure. It would take more than a millennium before Christian influences would be felt again.

With the arrival of European maritime powers in South India from the sixteenth century, a new wave of conversions to Christianity began. Most of India's Christian population resided in the southern half of the subcontinent. This was facilitated by the southern coast's historical exposure to foreign maritime influences which often included traders from Christian backgrounds. By the close of the 1700s the scene was set for the western powers. The Portuguese had a port at Goa in the south-west, and the French had Pondicherry in the south-east. The Dutch intermittently held Chinsura in the north-east, the Danes had small stations in Tranquebar in the south and Serampore in the north, and finally, the British were stationed in Bombay (Mumbai), Madras (Chennai) and Calcutta (Kolkata).[15] The Roman Catholic church's early entry into the field of evangelisation on the Indian subcontinent helped give it a dominant foothold in comparison with other Christian denominations. By 1700 an estimated two million people were Roman Catholic in India. The population of Christians in India stood at less than 1% in 1881 but had grown to 2.3% by 1951.

In Ceylon, Catholic conversions began from 1543 with the arrival of Franciscan monks and within a few decades they claimed to have a flock of approximately 52,000 people. By the end of the 1700s, Christianity, with Catholicism the dominant form, had a much stronger foothold in Ceylon than in mainland India, probably the result of stronger European political control in Ceylon. By 1881, almost 10% of the population was Christian.

With the opening of a British trading post on the island of Singapore in the 1820s, many saw new opportunities and arrived soon after. Among the Indians who arrived earliest in Singapore were many convicts from British colonial jails in India. Along with this group, there were free migrants who moved to the island, and these people do show up occasionally on church registers from 1840 onwards. Many of these free migrants were escaping economic hardship back in their home country. British colonial rule of India had made it effectively an economic vassal state of Britain. This process saw the conversion of India from an exporter of manufactured goods to a supplier of raw materials for Britain and an importer of British-made goods. Native Indian enterprises that competed against British interests were restrained and handicapped from the early nineteenth century. This impacted local commerce, manufacturing and shipping which had thrived for centuries. The decline of native Indian enterprises and businesses resulted in a reduction of occupational opportunities. Moreover, this curtailment of local industry contributed to the decline of smaller subsidiary and associated businesses. Potters, shoemakers, millers, and spinners all lost their traditional means of livelihood.[16] With shrinking opportunities, many of the old rich retreated to land ownership which in turn increased the pressure on small farmers. Landlords began demanding between 40 to 80% of their farm produce as 'rent'. Anyone unable to pay was forced off their land. The situation for wage earners was no better. Unemployment was high and pay was low.

*Tamil congregation at Penang's Church of St Francis Xavier, 1865*

Source: City Parish, Pulau Pinang

Even among the higher-caste groups, there were few employment opportunities. While the price of foodstuffs increased from 80 to 100% between 1888 and 1908, wages for government employees only rose by 30 to 50%.[17]

Many of the early Indian and Ceylonese Catholics were of South Indian origin, hailing from towns and villages near port cities such as Negapatam, with still others from further afield. They boarded ships for Singapore and Malaya. Some were already Catholic; the rest were converted in either the Malayan Archipelago or Singapore.

### The French, English, Irish and other Europeans

At an organisational, administrative, and even spiritual level, the early church was dominated by those of European descent. French priests from the MEP established and ran the missions. There was also a Spanish priest, Padre Anselmo Yegros, a rival Portuguese Mission missionary. Not welcomed into the fold of the local Portuguese Mission branch, he traipsed over to the rival French Mission in 1832, helping them set up their mission for a year. The remainder of this group were members of the laity who were active parishioners for the young church. Persons of Irish descent also figured prominently. Many were signatories to the original Singapore Catholic church building contract signed in December 1832. The most prominent of this group was Denis Lesley McSwiney, an Irishman. He arrived in Singapore in 1828 and worked as a clerk, merchant and contractor during his 20-year stay on the island. He is best remembered as the architect of the original Good Shepherd church (now Cathedral) in the 1840s. Other Irishmen, such as John Connolly and Joseph Melany, were shipping agents. Daniel Cunningham may have been a local police constable – his daughter Anna Theresa later married a Manila (Philippines) Spaniard in 1858. George Godfrey owned and ran a local tavern.

In social status terms, most of these parishioners did not belong to and could not identify with the British colonial elite. Firstly, they were Catholic, a Christian orientation deemed inferior by their Anglican and Protestant fellow Christians. Secondly, many were of Irish descent, a background despised by the English at that time. Many of these parishioners performed working-class to lower middle-class roles and occupations, working as clerks, policemen, small business owners, army or naval personnel, or tavern owners.

## References/Notes

[1] Kwa C.G, & Kua, B.L. (2019). *A General History of the Chinese in Singapore*. Singapore: World Scientific Publishing. p. 78.

[2] Cai, Xiang-yu. (2012). *Christianity and gender in South-East China: the choazhou missions (1849-1949)*. Doctoral dissertation: Universiteit Leiden. p. 4.

[3] Kwa & Kua. *Ibid*. pp. 6–7.

[4] Williams, K.M. (1976). *The Church in West Malaysia and Singapore: A study of the Catholic Church in West Malaysia and Singapore regarding her situation as an indigenous church*. Doctoral dissertation: Katholieke Universiteit Te Leuven. p. 93; Rerceretnam, M. (2011). *Black Europeans, the Indian Coolies and Empire: Colonialisation and Christianized Indians in colonial Malaya and Singapore, c. 1870s– c. 1950s*, Germany: VDM Verlag. pp. 49–50.

[5] Makepeace, W., Brooke, G.E., & Braddell, R. St. J. (1921/1991). *One Hundred Years of Singapore, Volume One*. Singapore: Oxford University Press. p. 235; Cook, J.A. Bethune. (1907). *Sunny Singapore: An Account of the place and its people, with a sketch of the results of missionary work*. London: Elliot Stock. p. 131.

[6] Buckley, C.B. (1902/1984). *An Anecdotal History of Old Times in Singapore: From foundation of the settlement under the honourable the East India Company on February 6th, 1819 to the transfer to the Colonial Office as part of the colonial possessions of the crown on April 1st, 1867*. Singapore: Oxford University Press. p. 242.

[7] Spanish Padre Anselmo Yegros was sent by the Portuguese Mission in Goa to Singapore to administer the Roman Catholic community; however, his already resident Portuguese counterpart, originally from Macao, refused to recognise his authority, and they parted ways. Padre Yegros appears to have struck up a friendship with the French mission and worked with them until his departure in early 1833.

[8] Rerceretnam, M. (2020). Intermarriage, religious conversions, and new Peranakans within multi-ethnic communities in colonial Singapore: The development of early multi-ethnic Roman Catholic communities, c. 1830s to 1860. In *Chapters on Asia (2019)*. Singapore: National Library Board.

[9] Cai, Xiang-yu. (2012). *Christianity and gender in South-East China: the choazhou missions (1849-1949)*. Doctoral dissertation: Universiteit Leiden. p. 28-29. Research continues and confirmation and geographical locations will be provided at a later date.

[10] Wright, N. (2019). Farquhar and Raffles: The Untold Story. In *Biblioasia*. Singapore: National Library Board. p. 5; Sng, B. (1980). In *His Good Time: The Story of the Church in Singapore, 1819–1978*. Singapore: Graduates' Christian Fellowship. p. 22;

Makepeace, W. (1921/1991). *One Hundred Years of Singapore, Volume One.* p. 343. Makepeace mistakenly attributes this initiative to Raffles.

11  Information from Vernon Adrian Emuang, community activist and founder of *Serani Sembang*. 2 July 202, citing Margaret Sarkissian (2021), *Ripples across Time and Space: The Malaysian Rancho Folclorico tradition.* Conference paper. Sarkissian claims how Portuguese dances and other culture were only introduced into Melaka in the early 1950s. Sarkissian, M. (2005). Being Portuguese in Malacca: The Politics of Folk Culture in Malaysia. Etnografica, Vol. IX (1). p. 167-8.

12  Interview with Vicky Rodrigues and Valerie Scully. Interviewed by Marc Rerceretnam, 16 January 2020.

13  Rerceretnam, M. (2011). *Black Europeans, the Indian Coolies and Empire: Colonialisation and Christianized Indians in colonial Malaya and Singapore, c. 1870s–c. 1950s.* Saarbrücken, Germany: VDM Verlag Dr Müller. p. 33.

14  Ibid, p. 34.
15  Ibid, p. 35.
16  Ibid, p. 37.
17  Ibid, p. 39.

Chapter 2

# The Multiracial Landscape of Early Singapore

The Roman Catholic church, led by the French missionary organisation MEP, set up a permanent base in Singapore in 1832. At this time, Catholic worshippers on the island numbered approximately 300 people.[1] The majority were mixed-blood descendants of the Portuguese from Melaka, many of whom were recent arrivals. However, the church was also beginning to make headway with conversions in the Teochew migrant community from the eastern region of China's Guangdong province, the earliest of these emerging in August 1833.[2]

Catholic Church archives show most of the early lay congregation was made up of Melakans. They most likely started to arrive soon after the establishment of the colonial outpost of Singapore, beginning from about June 1819. It is difficult to corroborate the numbers, as the church did not keep statistics or lists of congregation members at the time. However, marriage and baptism records from the period do show the Melakan community accounting for more than half of all marriage and baptism ceremonies between 1832 and 1843, ahead of the second most significant group, the Teochews, and followed to a lesser extent by Indians, Eurasians from Penang, India, or Bencoolen, and finally, Europeans, including those from the British Isles. There do not seem to have been any locally born ethnic or Peranakan Chinese, or Indians, in this early congregation. Tamils, mainly from Madras, began to appear in the congregation from early 1840.

## Establishment of the Roman Catholic church

When the Portuguese brought Christianity to the Malay Archipelago via their invasion of Melaka in 1511, the new religion had little effect on local populations in the region. Their ongoing disputes with neighbouring states, disinterest in evangelisation and their brutality against and mistreatment of native populations, did not entice others to convert to their religion.[4] That changed slightly after the British established their trading post in Penang in 1786, and later, in Singapore in 1819. The first Roman Catholic chapel in Singapore was consecrated on 5 May 1833, located on the site of today's Singapore Art Museum (the former St Joseph's Institution [1852–1988] or SJI school building) on Bras Basah Road, where French Catholic missionaries had been granted rent-free land by the British colonial government in 1832 (see Chapter 1). The chapel was dedicated to both the Good Shepherd and St Francis Xavier. The modestly designed chapel measured a mere 18.3 metres by 9 metres.[5] Between 1832 and 1839, the congregation grew relatively quickly,

*The Church of the Good Shepherd (later Cathedral), c. 1860s*

Source: St Joseph's Institution archives

especially after the appointment of China-born Father John Tschu, whose ministry had made inroads into the local Teochew community. This resulted in the conversion of large numbers of China-born Teochew settlers. With steady growth came a need to expand beyond the little chapel, and by 1841 fundraising for a much larger church had begun.[6] The Church of the Good Shepherd building was completed six years later, in 1847. In the previous year, another church, St Joseph's, had been built in the rural Bukit Timah district, catering to large communities of Teochew workers and planters living in the area.[7]

The French mission was not the first Catholic group to establish itself in Singapore. Back in 1825, the Macao (Macau) arm of the Portuguese Mission had sent Padre Francisco de Silva e Maia to set up a permanent base in Singapore. However, the Mission made no effort to support this sole priest to build a church. Hence Padre Maia's role remained minor. In addition, the Portuguese Mission's mindset was different from that of the French. The Mission had been in the region since the fall of the Melaka Sultanate to the Portuguese in 1511. Because the triumphant Portuguese did not endear themselves to the local population, Christianity remained within the limited confines of the resident Melaka Portuguese population. This 300-year-old mindset was still in place when the Mission set itself up in Singapore in 1825. It made no attempt to reach out beyond its own congregation, and also appeared to be poorly managed. In 1832, the Goa-based arm of the Mission sent Padre Anselmo Yegros to Singapore to administer the Catholic community, unaware that their Macao counterparts had already sent Padre Francisco de Silva e Maia seven years earlier. Demonstrating the high level of rivalry, hostility, and ineptitude within the Mission, the already resident Padre Maia refused to recognise newcomer Padre Yegros, who was then forced to take refuge with the French Mission until his departure from Singapore in early 1833. From the 1830s onwards, the animosity between the Portuguese and the French Mission remained a sore point for many decades. The Portuguese claimed ecclesiastical control of the region, but the issue was only resolved in 1886, in the French Mission's favour.[8]

By the late 1830s, the resident French priest, realising the huge evangelical potential of the resident Teochew community, recruited the services of a native Teochew-speaker, Father John Tschu. Tschu was brought to Singapore expressly to evangelise among the local Teochew community. Born in Canton in the 1790s, he had done his clerical training in Penang and was later ordained in Siam. In 1838, he was appointed as head of the Chinese Mission in Singapore. Unfortunately, Tschu died suddenly in 1848 and was buried at the cemetery of St Joseph's Church in Mandai (his remains were moved later to Bukit Timah, with the church itself). It was largely due to his efforts that the local Teochew congregation saw substantial growth in the 1840s.

## Conversion – the Chinese community

When the Roman Catholic church was established in Singapore in 1832, its resident community was not known for its recent converts. About 90% of the approximately 300-strong congregation comprised Melaka Portuguese, longstanding or born Catholics, albeit only recent arrivals to Singapore from Melaka. The rest were English-speaking, Eurasians mainly from Penang, Bencoolen and Madras, with a handful of English, Irish, and a few more Europeans. However, the French priests in the MEP were resolute about evangelising to non-Catholics. They were usually at least familiar with, or even trained in specific languages, in keeping with the mother-tongues of their intended flocks. Resident priests Fathers Étienne Albrand (1805–1853) and Jean-Baptiste Boucho (1797–1871) were not proficient in the Chinese dialects of Teochew or Hokkien, but relied on a catechist to make themselves understood.[9] On 18 August 1833, Francis Ah Fa (aged thirty-five), Francis Ah Li (thirty-six), Joseph Ah Hee (twenty-nine) and Vincent Ah Kiau (thirty-one) were baptised by Father Albrand. Obviously friends, the men were all baptised in a single ceremony.[10]

Religious conversion typically spreads along familial and communal lines. Hence, the first converts in Singapore almost exclusively came from one dialect group or several villages. There is growing evidence showing that there was a small number of Hakkas within this early congregation too. This was the case from the 1830s until around the 1880s or 1890s, when Cantonese began joining the church. Hokkiens joined in the

*Bishop Jean Baptiste Boucho (1797-1871)*
Source: Chancery of the Roman Catholic Archdiocese of Singapore

immediate decades after the 1900s. Research for this book shows that Singapore's Teochew Catholics originated from either southern China's Huilai county (Catholic since the 1700s) or nearby Shantou/Swatow (汕头市).[11] Some Cantonese may have come from Catholic villages such as Siu Heng/Cuiheng (翠亨村) about 26 kilometres north of Macau.[12]

One personal account of religious conversion in China in the 1860s sheds some light. Chia Hack Boo and his new wife were from the Shantou village of Longhuizen (龙湖镇). They were friends with another couple from a neighbouring village called Swalek/Xianlecun (仙乐), a few kilometres south of their village. This Swalek couple, from the Low clan, had recently converted to Roman Catholicism, following their two elder brothers, Benedict and Jacobe Low, who converted in Singapore in 1863 under the auspices of the MEP mission on River Valley Road. According to Low family records, the young Low couple were probably David Low Kiok Liang and his wife Maria Tan. Unfortunately, there was considerable opposition within both the Chia and Low clans to their conversion, with the young couples moving to Bangkok soon after.[13]

Nevertheless, it is highly probable that most of the Singapore church population was converted on the island, not in China. Evangelisation, the influence of family networks, placement under the care of church orphanages, changes in personal outlook, or the loss of faith in one's former religion were among the many strong reasons for conversion to Christianity.

For the early Teochew convert back in the 1830s, 1840s or 1850s, the conversion process was not a straightforward exercise. As Taoists, conversion for the Teochews meant renouncing membership of their clan or *kongsi* (cooperative economic and cultural unions, sometimes secret societies). Thus these organisations would view a member's conversion as an insult, an intrusion, and a threat to their domain. To fellow clan leaders and members, giving up one's Taoist beliefs seemed a serious move. As observed in the early 1830s:

> *The Chinese in Singapore usually belong to a secret society, like the Freemasons, which makes their conversion to Christianity more difficult. The heads of the secret societies are very much against Christians.*
>
> Annals of the Propagation of the Faith, XLII, 10 September 1833.

Taoists venerate their ancestors. The abandonment of such practices after becoming Christian was viewed as sacrilege. Within a month of the first conversions in August 1833, there were reports of clan intimidation against Father Albrand while he was doing his rounds in Singapore city.

> *During the day, my Catechist and I go around to speak to the pagans to ask them to come, and sometimes, we have the happiness of seeing them come in the evening for instruction. But sadly, I can only speak a few words of their language, and of one language only, the one of my catechists. I know neither of the Fokkien (Hokkien) or the Tchang-*

*Tcheou (Teochew) which is spoken by two-thirds of the Chinese people in Singapore.*

Annals of the Propagation of the Faith, XLII, 10 September 1833.

Conflicts within clan territories were common. Members who found themselves in conflict with, or in dispute with the clan or its hierarchy, often migrated to Johore (Johor) on the southern Malayan peninsula, to escape clan control.[14] Many new converts abhorred the clans. Father Albrand wrote of local Teochews:

*Here they have no fear of the Mandarin or their brothers. They live here in the protection of a government, tolerant by politics. When they encounter injustices, they come to me and I help and protect them like the government. My contact opened their eyes to see the light of truth.*

Annals of the Propagation of the Faith, XLII, 26 December 1833.

With regards to 'government' protection, there seems to have been at least one parishioner, Daniel Cunningham, who may have been a constable in the police force at the time.[15] He probably helped with police matters. Teochew converts often referred to their former clan leaders as the 'head of the devil'. In August or September 1833, a new convert was reported to have defiantly said:

*We chose the camaraderie of this faith; we do not fear you. When we return to China, we will be Christians. And if we are killed, we will go to heaven. As for the pigtail, and our Chinese clothes, you can take them off and you can cut our heads and tear our skin. By harming us, you make us very happy.*

Annals of the Propagation of the Faith, XLII, 10 September 1833.

Many of these converts intermarried with local non-Teochew Roman Catholic women.[16] To an extent, the move to convert and marry outside their own Teochew community bears testimony to the strength of their identification with their new religion, outstripping old racial or cultural boundaries and alliances. It suggests an openness to their new multiracial

Singaporean environment, even an acceptance of modernity, and of an entrée to a larger globalising world. These men realised they were no longer living in an isolated village environment and saw their situation as a new road leading to new opportunities in a new future.

*A multiracial Catholic family c. 1877. Melaka-born Yeo Gek Neo (seated left) with Shantou-born husband Goh Choon Hin (seated right), with their non-Chinese in-law Anna Maria Blanco and her new husband Shantou-born John Goh Ah Seng (both standing right)*

Source: Goh family descendants

The French Mission's evangelical undertaking did not end with the newly converted Teochews. While the numbers were small in comparison, early church archives do provide a record of other converts from different backgrounds, many non-Christian in origin. These were largely Malay Muslims, Hindu Indians or even aboriginal *Orang Asli* natives of the region. This was especially so from the 1860s onwards, many first arriving in Singapore via the orphanage of the Convent of the Holy Infant Jesus (CHIJ) located on Victoria Street.

## Conversion – Melaka Portuguese, Eurasians and Malays

Of all the Asian communities in Singapore, the Melaka Portuguese were by far the earliest converts to Catholicism. They are linked with events following the Portuguese invasion of Melaka and expulsion of the ruling Sultanate in 1511. The heritage of this community is multifaceted and complicated.[17] With the capture and occupation of Melaka, a new community was born to local women and Portuguese fathers. The occupational force was not solely Portuguese: a third of the 1,400-strong invasion force were of Goan descent. In addition, Melaka had long been a cosmopolitan trading post hosting local communities and travellers both, from India, China, and the Middle East. Resident Peranakan communities such as not only the Peranakan Chinese but also the Chettis (or 'Chitty Melaka' – Malayanised Tamil Indians) were well established at the time of the Melaka Sultanate. All these admixtures would have been incorporated into the general genetic makeup of the various Melakan communities, including the *mestizo* Melaka Portuguese group. Christianity's introduction into Melaka, unlike the generally peaceful coexistence of first Hinduism then Islam, was more militaristic and violent at its inception. The Portuguese found themselves often at war with the neighbouring sultanates of Johore and Acheh (Aceh). They were ruthless in their handling of local communities.

This attitude helped pit Islam against Christianity in the region and made the predominantly Muslim Malays antagonistic towards anything Christian. William Milne (1795–1822), a missionary with the London Missionary Society (LMS), made a curious observation in 1820. He noted the disillusionment of the Malay Muslim population towards Christians in the colony. He described the 'avarice, lying, and cozening which appear in carrying on commerce; the drunkenness, loose morals, and hardness of heart towards slaves, which have at times been manifested by the professors of the gospel, have steeled the Musselman's soul against Christianity'.[18] In another account, one of the first MEP missionaries to land in Singapore, Father Mathurin-Pierre Pécot, was met with hostile men wielding their fearsome traditional wavy-bladed *kris* knives when he tried to evangelise at a Malay village in November 1821.[19] Based on

Catholic church baptism records, there is little evidence of Muslim Malay conversion.[20] Prior to the 1870s, some Christian missionaries did evangelise in Malay communities but with very little success.[21] By the 1870s, to placate the interests of various Malay state sultans, the British colonial authorities decided to discourage such practices.

*St Joseph's Church (Portuguese Mission) was built in 1853*

Source: Chancery of the Roman Catholic Archdiocese of Singapore

Consequently, Christianity did not take root in the local Malay community. This Malay community was well established within an old social structure, and it was highly unlikely that any community member would be enticed to venture outside of this protective structure. Christianity in Melaka did not spread beyond the confines of the small community of Melaka Portuguese descendants. It was only after British interests began infiltrating the Malay Archipelago in the 1700s that new initiatives in Christian evangelisation began, and then only via new non-Muslim immigrant arrivals. By 1876, with the signing of the Treaty of Pangkor between the British and the Malay chiefs of Perak state, new resolutions designed to placate state sultans were put in place. One of these gave full authority to the Muslim religion and customary norms. As a result, strict rules on the conversion of Muslims were embedded in the various 'School Codes' then in force. Legally there was no state legislation which prevented the conversion of Muslims to another faith; however, colonial policy discouraged such conversions, and Christian religious institutions appeared to toe the line without question.[22]

With the arrival of the British and other European traders into the region in the late 1700s, informal or *de facto* sexual relationships with local women were formed. The resultant offspring seeded a small community of Eurasians. While Singapore also had its own fair share of such liaisons, in the first few decades following 1819, many first- or second-generation Eurasians moved to Singapore from places like Penang, Bencoolen and Madras.[23]

## Conversion – South Asian community

Numerous conversions were recorded in Singapore and the Malay states in the nineteenth and early twentieth centuries. For example, personal accounts are on record telling of how a young boy helped convert an elderly neighbour, or a young girl led into prostitution who asks police for help and is admitted to an orphanage; or the case of a man who converts and writes back to his wife and family in India about his conversion, whereupon his family follows suit and converts. For Hindus, reasons to convert did not need always to be religious or spiritual in nature, as most were not hostile to other religions, with many viewing these religions as offering new 'deities' that enriched their own spiritual landscape.[24] Many Hindus did not object to being preached to by Christians, but took offence only when told that Jesus Christ was the only god.[25]

It is difficult to pinpoint the first Catholics of South Asian or Indian origin in Singapore. There is a strong possibility a handful may have existed in the early 1830s, within the early Bras Basah Road congregation, but records are inconclusive. Around late June 1833, a Bengali man was baptised and named James Jacob. He was about 28-years-old. There is a strong possibility such early converts were inmates from the new prison, located nearby. Records on these are rare, but these very early converts may have been awaiting execution and baptised just before their deaths.

The earliest marriage record appears on 12 February 1840. A 28-year-old Malabar-born, Malayalee man named Rochus married a 16-year-old Malayalee woman named Anna. They both appear to already be Catholics. The South Asian congregation would later share churches with their fellow Catholic Teochew parishioners between 1870 till 1888, after which a new church, The Church of Our Lady of Lourdes, was opened in Ophir Road.

Historically, Indian/Hindu conversion to Catholicism has been underestimated. There is strong evidence demonstrating a high rate of conversion to Catholicism among rubber plantation-based Indians in Malaya. There is also evidence showing that most Catholic immigrants had already been converted to the faith in India.[26] This may have been so for the urbanised, middle-class group, but the high levels of Malayan plantation-based conversions show that there was a considerable pool of non-Christian people in Malaya who were receptive to conversion. Data retrieved from Kuala Lumpur's Church of St Anthony between 1891 and 1950 show that out of the 1,339 marriages celebrated, there were over 410 individuals (30.62%) who had converted to Catholicism. The vast majority of these were the product of marriages between Catholics and Hindus. However, rivalries among church groups were strong, especially between Catholic and Protestant groups. Therefore, most social and religious interaction among the different groups was frowned upon by Catholic and Protestant clergy alike.[27] In Kuala Lumpur and Selangor, Catholic conversions of Protestants were extremely rare, with only four recorded accounts (three Methodists and one Anglican). There were also three converts from Islam.[28] In Singapore the numbers were slightly higher, with ten conversions from Protestantism between 1884 and 1895.[29]

Back in India, higher-caste Christian converts were often ostracised by their families and communities. However, religious differences between Hindus and converts were non-existent among the 'Untouchable' caste groups. There appeared to be a stronger emphasis on ethnicity than on religion. In the 1950s, an Indian Protestant missionary noted how willingly Indian Catholics introduced them to their fellow Indian Roman Catholic friends, 'not because we were Christian workers, but because Mr Verghese and I were Indians', he claimed.[30] If any reservations did exist, they were seen mainly in a political light, not from a religious perspective.[31]

Indian migration to Singapore and Malaya only began in earnest with the expansion of the rubber industry from the 1890s, and especially from the 1900s. Most of these migrants worked the newly established rubber plantations, while a smaller number, who were English language-educated, worked in white-collar jobs, mainly in administrative roles in government service.

*Our Lady of Lourdes Church was built in 1888 for the Indian congregation*
Source: Chancery of the Roman Catholic Archdiocese of Singapore

In the Catholic church, the lower castes Pallan, Paraiyar, Valangai and Vanniyar, as well as the Shanar/Nadar caste group, made up about 80% of the church population. The rest were identified as high-caste Vellalar, Naidu, Chetty, Mudaliyar and Agambadiar caste groups. To an extent, these higher-caste groups were endogamous and probably operated at times as a larger single high-caste bloc. The slightly lower-caste Odaiyar/Vanniyar groups were occasionally accepted into the high-caste fold, on the proviso that the preconditions of a suitable educational background, occupational status and the social suitability of the family had been met. Religious conversion among members of the highest-ranking caste, the Brahmin group, was extremely rare. Few people of this caste ever migrated to Singapore or the Malay Archipelago.

According to old Indian parishioners, Catholic clergy banned formal caste practices within their congregations. Even parishioners among the higher-caste groups, who were least likely to drop caste prejudices, spoke of caste's declining importance.[32] Consequently caste delineations for the many Indian Catholics grew increasingly vague from generation to generation.[33] In the past, like their Chinese-dialect group and clan-based counterparts, the castes had tended to marry within their own groups, but marriages began to diversify beyond these boundaries in the decades following the Second World War. After the 1920s and 1930s, more importance was attached to a person's occupational and educational status, or personal demeanour, rather than to his/her traditional caste status.

## Strategic omissions and the adoption of new names

From the 1830s or 1840s, Chinese clan organisations established themselves in several ways. Membership of a clan organisation was determined by one's ancestry tracing to a specific village or neighbouring villages. In other cases, it was simply determined by an individual's surname. Because of the strong animosity between the clan and *kongsi* organisations and many Catholic converts, it is not surprising that Chinese converts appeared unwilling to use their clan names in everyday activity.[34] Church archival records clearly show a consistent trend where Teochew men did not provide their clan names, hence many of their names contained only their newly adopted Christian name plus their Chinese given name. For example, Joseph 'A' Hee' (*sic* in the records) appeared to drop his surname/clan name when he got married in May

1834. Likewise, 'Pedro' included only his given Chinese name Nong Keah (奴仔 – written as 'Ano Kigna') when he married in September 1841. Such examples dominate church registers and appear to show how Singapore's Teochew converts were unwilling to identify themselves via their clan names, probably because of these names' negative associations with the old clan organisations. However, it is interesting to note that when their signatures were required, many would still include their clan names, but only when signing in Chinese script. They did not include their westernised Christian names when doing this. This practice continued until around 1858, when parishioners began to use their clan names even in church circles.

Noteworthy too is the number of China-born Teochew men who adopted popular Portuguese variations of Christian names. 'Domingo', 'Pedro', 'Joao', 'Joachim' and 'Peter de Santa Maria' are a few examples adopted by new converts between the 1830s and 1850s. Such names quite clearly indicate a close social relationship enjoyed between many Teochew men and members of the Melaka Portuguese community within the church.

Another point worth noting is the low social standing of many of these early Teochew migrants. Using Pedro Tan Nong Keah (陳奴仔) as an example, his given name 'Nong Keah' (奴仔) translates into 'slave' or 'child' in the English language, with a hint of being a worthless female too. This was clearly an informal child's nickname, meant to be modest and humbly belittling of oneself. There were many other adult parishioners with similar childhood nicknames, later used formally in adult life, like 'Ah Kau' (dog), 'Ah Tee' (little boy) and 'Ah Soi' (small one) – often, the more dismissive, demeaning, or ugly the nickname was, the better, as it was sometimes meant to deter malevolent forces from finding the child attractive enough to steal or harm. In more well-to-do, privileged or educated families, a child would be renamed in his/her late teens in a special 'Walk out of the garden' (出花园) coming-of-age ceremony, when he/she would be given an adult name to replace their old 'childish' name. In Tan's case, he was not afforded this privilege. This was probably because his standing in the family was low, or more likely because he was adopted into the Tan clan/family and was therefore not regarded as biological family, rather deemed an outsider and so not afforded such familial privileges.

In the South Asian community too, before conversion, especially among the lower-caste groups, names were traditionally used to reflect low status or to denote servility and dependence.[35] Many saw conversion and a name change as a clear psychological break from their low status. The choice of a new name often denoted their strong desire to improve their own situation and that of their family and community. For the higher-caste groups and the more well-to-do converts, adoption of a Christian name conjured similar sentiments,[36] but with a colonial 'upgrading' twist.

South Asian/ Indian names were constructed primarily in two ways. Firstly, a person could keep his/her father's name as their own, which was more traditional. Secondly, one could adopt the European tradition of keeping the patrilineal name. These two styles were especially common among Catholic Indian communities.[37] From church records, it is clear that most names before the late 1920s and early 1930s comprised mainly the first category (father's name adopted as part of the new name). Thus, a parishioner would have their own baptismal name, for example 'John', while their father's name was 'Arokiasamy'. Hence 'John (son of) Arokiasamy' or 'John Arokiasamy'. The next generation would then use 'John' as their last name, and so on.

The European tradition of maintaining a more consistently patrilineal surname became common after the late 1920s and early 1930s, and then mainly in the urban middle class, particularly for those in clerical or white-collar occupations.[38] This was especially common with Malayali parishioners (of south Indian descent, Kerala state). The choice of a baptismal name was often regulated by one's parish priest.[39] By convention no names honouring Hindu deities were allowed, but 'Indianised' Christian names were acceptable. The use of such Indian Christian names was especially common up to the first two or three decades of the twentieth century, mostly among recent arrivals from India. For example, 'Sinnapur' is Paul, 'Soosay' is Joseph, 'Yagappar' is James, and 'Erayapan' is Peter.[40] The choice of names also corresponded with the popularity of particular saints.[41]

Many of these uniquely Indianised names had direct or indirect connections with the church, often reconstructed from Hindu nomenclature. The name 'Kolandasamy' when broken down means 'Koland' (baby) and 'Samy' (god), or 'Baby of God'. Likewise, a name like 'Mariadass' is a veneration of the Virgin Mary, from 'Maria' (Mary) and 'Dass' (servant), or 'Servant of the Virgin Mary'. Certain names were used more regularly in some churches than others. For example, names ending with 'samy' tended to be Catholic.[42] Names honouring popular saints such as St Francis Xavier, St Anne, St Anthony, or even religious occurrences such as at the apparitions of the Virgin Mary in Lourdes (France), were popular with Catholic parishioners.

Over time, names not originally used as patrilineal surnames were gradually used as such. Examples of such names are Saverimuthu, Lazarus, Peter, Pragasam, Manuel, Joseph, Louis, Kolandasamy, Doraisamy, Ponnusamy, George, David, Anthony, Lourdes, Mariadass, Jesudass, Gnanamuthu, Sebastian and Aloysius. Female names were always used as first names, strung onto their father's name or patrilineal surname. Examples of female names are Saveriammal, Salome, Anna, Rose, Grace, Lily, Agnes, Anthoniammal, Lourdamal, Annammal, Mary, Elizabeth, Jessy, Ruby, Violet and Mariammal.

Among the mainly urban-based and white-collar Malayali communities (who originally had been converted under Portuguese rule in the 1500s)[43] names such as Gomez, Pereira, D'Cruz, Fernandez (and to a lesser extent Netto, Lobo, Lopez, Miranda, D'Cunha, Morais and Mendez)[44] were commonly used as surnames. The use of Portuguese first names was still prevalent in the late nineteenth century. However, in keeping with these Malayali Christians' primarily English-educated backgrounds, by the late nineteenth century there was an apparent shift towards more Anglicised first names such as Walter, Edward, Richard, Frederick, Edwin, Lawrence, or other popular Anglicised biblical names. These Malayali communities however maintained the use of their Portuguese surnames.[45]

Caste titles, especially those belonging to the higher-caste groups such as the Vellalars, Mudaliyars, Odaiyar (Reddiar), Nairs and Pillais, were in some cases maintained as patrilineal surnames, provoking some speculation that persons from these higher caste groups deliberately retained their caste names to maintain their status.[46] Judging by the available church records however, this was not necessarily true. Most high-caste Catholics had dropped their caste titles in favour of conventional Christian surnames by the early twentieth century. Setting aside the possible impact of discouragement from some churches (particularly Protestant ones), it seems that the use of a caste title very much depended on how much the title meant to the title-holder himself, or on how 'Europeanised' he or she had become.

## Intermarriage within the Catholic church

Back in the 1830s and 1840s, the new Catholic community must have appeared to be a relatively unique experiment in social and cultural mixing, to clergy, parishioners, and outsiders alike. The mix between local-born and overseas-born, racial groups and different languages, made the newly consecrated chapel on Bras Basah Road resemble a miniature Tower of Babel. It seems unlikely that we will ever know the exact relationships between the different racial and cultural communities. They can be broken up into five distinct groups: Southeast Asian, Melaka Portuguese, East Asian, South Asian, and Eurasian. There were undeniable divisions within these groups, aligned with wealth and class. Few attempted to cross the social barriers or defy the negative racial stereotypes that existed at the time. While relationships would have been superficially cordial it was highly unlikely that a layperson of European background would voluntarily mix socially with people they perceived as their social inferiors. However, there were exceptions to this rule. Certain community groups, although culturally very different, were open to friendships with other groups. One such group was the numerically dominant Melaka Portuguese community, who appeared to be extremely friendly with newly arrived China-born Teochew migrants.

Intermarriage can be viewed as a key indicator of social integration. A high level of intermarriage indicates a strong level of social interaction in the general community, across racial, cultural, religious and lingual lines. Over a twenty-five-year period, between 1833 and 1858, there was a total of 125 marriages celebrated under the auspices of the French mission of the Catholic church in Singapore. Of this number, forty-two, or 33.6% of marriages involved mixed-race couples. This is significant in Singaporean, or for that matter Malaysian history, as no other culturally and racially diverse community is known to have existed within colonial Singapore at the time. These early marriages were probably directly arranged and negotiated by two parties; the bride's family and the prospective groom. Men would have had the final say in these matchmaking decisions, since colonial society was strongly patriarchal.

Colonialism's implied racial hierarchy was based on the idea that some races were superior to others, and it also incorporated strong gender overtones. Under these circumstances, cultural differences within the church played only a minor role; rather, the commonalities of a shared new religious faith strengthened and united the seemingly disparate groups within the local church community. No official statistics are available on the size of these early congregations, but estimates do exist. In 1833, a year after the establishment of the Catholic mission on Bras Basah Road, the congregation was assessed to be around 300. By 1851, this had climbed marginally to 340 (150 of whom were located at the Bukit Timah church site). Between 1833 and 1846, within the China-born community, there were eight marriages, which means that many more did not get the opportunity to marry.[47]

At the time, the Melaka Portuguese community was divided into two clear social groups, (see Chapter 1). The 'Upper Tens' who mostly claimed Dutch or British heritage, were literate in English, and held white-collar jobs.

While delineations and discrimination may have existed within the old Melaka Portuguese community, the essential concept of 'race' and identity was still reasonably open. There is clear evidence some families within the community appeared to accept all people, regardless of race, into their family fold. Clear examples can be seen within some 'Upper Ten' families. On the 6$^{th}$ of April 1833, the following people were baptised:

> A 30-year-old Sarawak born man from the Niah clan, baptised and renamed Joseph da Costa. His godparents were (Cyprus?) de Costa and Victoria Fernandez.

A 24-year-old East Malaysian (natione Timor Malanesem) was baptised and renamed Lawrence Jansen. His godparent was Felix Jansen.

A 32-year-old man described as being of 'Batta Malanesem' background is baptised and renamed Peter Woodford. Godparents were J Woodford and Hyacinth Fernandez.

A 38-year-old Malay woman (natione Malanesem) is baptised and renamed Susan Meoem Paschalis Doral. Godparents were Nicholas de Olivero and (Christina?) Godfrey.

A 30-year-old Javanese woman (natione natum Java Malanesem) is baptised and renamed Carolina De Costa. Godmother was Martha Francis.

An 18-year-old Chinese man, born in China, is baptised and renamed Joachin Peiro. Godparents Sebastian (?) and Anna Louisa.

At least six more Malay and East Malaysian individuals were baptised between 1833 and 1834. However, they were excluded from this list because their names were partially undecipherable.

On the other hand, there were the poor and largely illiterate Kristang creole-speaking 'Portuguese' who made up the lower class, mostly fishermen.[48] Being poor, it is hardly surprising that many of these Melaka Portuguese eagerly seized any opportunity to align themselves with potentially promising China-born men, including well-to-do merchants. Matches between these two groups seemed a good fit. Conversely, there were no marriages between members of the 'Upper Tens' and China-born Teochew men, whom the 'Upper Tens' most likely regarded as their social inferiors. Similarly, no European woman ever married an Asian man.

If they wanted to get married in Singapore, the options were bleak for many China-born Teochew men. New immigrants did not have a social network in Singapore. So, in order to seek a spouse, they had to take time away from employment and travel back to China, an extremely expensive exercise. The other option was to find an appropriate and willing partner locally. Marrying a local woman was made more difficult by the low ratio of women to men. In 1823, the ratio of women to men in the Malayan archipelago was 1:8, by 1850 1:12, and in 1860 1:15. These numbers were echoed in Singapore with one Chinese woman to fifteen Chinese men in the mid-1860s, improving slightly in the 1880s to 1:9. This demographic obstacle to marriage therefore was not unique to the Catholic community.[49]

Similar dynamics could be observed at the rural St Joseph's Church Teochew community located at Bukit Timah. A large majority of this community consisted of poor farmers, offering no financial enticement for potential brides. Overall, there were a mere seventy-one marriages recorded in this parish between 1847 and 1880. As a Catholic, the only viable option for matrimonial bliss was with a fellow Catholic. Marriage under the auspices of the church would not allow marriage with a non-believer (barring exceptional cases); marriages with Protestants were tolerated occasionally, but only after the Protestant partner had signed an oath to allow their Catholic partner to continue as a Catholic and to bring up their children as such. In Singapore, seeking spouses within the resident Peranakan Chinese community was not an option for other Chinese. For this period (1830s–1860s), there is no available evidence indicating a pre-existing Catholic Chinese Peranakan community in Singapore. Even if such a community did exist, Peranakan Chinese were unlikely to accept lowly China-born *sinkeh* (i.e. 'new arrivals', new blood) within their ranks. Exceptions were made only if a *sinkeh* was regarded as especially industrious or possessing special potential.50

The earliest record of a Catholic marriage involving a China-born Teochew male is dated 22 May 1834. On this day, Joseph A' He (one of the original converts of 18 August 1833) married a young Melaka Portuguese woman named Magdalene Panna. More followed in the coming decades. A picture of the early Catholic church from the 1830s onwards would have told a fascinating visual story. A large proportion of married couples were in interracial marriages. They and their racially mixed children on the way to church on Sundays would have been a striking image, foreshadowing modern multiracial Singapore by over a century.

## Singapore's first homegrown Peranakan bloodline

Song Ong Siang's seminal 1923 book on the Chinese communities of Singapore, *One Hundred Years' History of the Chinese in Singapore*, correctly observed that the majority of Singapore Peranakan families went back only three or four generations from their original source, usually a 'pure' Chinese progenitor from China.[51] Significantly, these early intermarriages between Melaka-Portuguese, Malay and Indigenous women and China-born men are therefore the start of a Singapore-specific Peranakan bloodline. This is based on the current understanding of how a 'Peranakan' is defined: by the union of a local-born with an overseas-born spouse or partner.[52] For example, between the 22 May 1834 and October 1870 there were 26 first generation China-born with local-born Peranakan marriages. They were mostly (but not exclusively) China-born males to local-born females:[53]

| | |
|---|---|
| 22.5.1834 | Joseph A'He (China) & Magdalene Panna (Melaka) |
| 22.1.1835 | Stephen A'Tcho (China) & Eugenia Pedro (Melaka) |
| 10.9.1837 | Vincent A'Kim (China) & Mariam (Melaka) |
| 30.6.1841 | Joachim A'Siva (China) & J. Da Costa (Singapore) |
| 6.9.1841 | Pedro A'No Kia (China) & Joanna An Gau (Singapore) |
| 18.10.1841 | You Tchou (China) & Dominique Sybra |
| 10.7.1843 | Anthony A'Kou & Joanna Monteiro (Melaka) |
| 30.7.1844 | Francis Appa (China) & Jenk Tons (Melaka) |
| 7.1.1846 | A'Kiau (China) & Mariam Manip |
| 4.11.1846 | A'Choun (China) & Pon-Pon (Rhio) |
| 24.11.1846 | Allay (China) & Silbero (Singapore) |
| 9.11.1847 | A'Poin (China) & Catherine Bouna |
| 15.2.1848 | Chau bourne (China) & Sequiera (Singapore) |
| 11.9.1849 | Andrew No Kigha (China) & Maria Ling What (Lingga) |
| 23.7.1850 | Peter de Santa Maria (China) & Elizabeth Rozelles (Penang) |
| 29.7.1850 | Ambrose Hiang A'Chin (China) & Philomena Siam Hiaw (Melaka) |
| 19.11.1850 | Chin-nam (China) & Rosal (Melaka) |
| 8.9.1851 | F. Siu Tae Tsaun (China) & Catherine Simon (Singapore) |
| 28.4.1852 | Matthew Ngah Pingan (China) & Maria Lyehouse (Penang) |
| 4.11.1852 | Thaddoum Akau (China) Cecilia Simon (Melaka) |

| | |
|---|---|
| 24.1.1855 | Paul Tan Yong (China) & Marcella (Penang) |
| 26.6.1855 | Simon A'Naw (China) & Alberque (Melaka) |
| 26.9.1855 | Laurence Lee Chan (China) & Rosa Maria Beseh (Melaka) |
| 30.1.1858 | John Yan-Kauh (China) & Maria (Borneo) |
| 31.1.1867 | Peter Tseng Ah Tuane (China) & Leonora Aroozoo (Singapore) |
| 10.1870 | Antoni Goon A Khit (China) & Angelica David d/o David (Melaka)[54] |

Source: *Good Shepherd Cathedral and St Joseph's Church (Bukit Timah) Marriage registers*

Peranakan communities arguably have existed in the wider East Asian region since the tenth century, but only from the sixteenth–eighteenth centuries in the Malay Archipelago region.[55] Jawi Peranakan (Arab-Malay), Chetti Peranakan (Indian-Malay), Kristang Peranakan (Melaka Portuguese) and lastly, Hokkien Peranakan communities, were already long established in the region when Raffles and Farquhar landed in Singapore in 1819. With overseas-local marriages taking place from 1834, these mixed marriages came to account for a significant proportion of the new Catholic community. Between the years 1834 and the late 1850s, there were an estimated twenty-five mixed marriages.[56]

Catholic marriages among the smaller groups, such as Eurasians, Indians, and Europeans, shared different dynamics. The more recent Eurasian communities (1700s–1800s) which developed in places like Penang, Madras and Bencoolen, were generally a result of informal liaisons between local women and European colonial civil servants, soldiers, or traders. In Singapore, early Eurasian marriages (1833–1843) seem to have aimed mainly at pairing off fellow Eurasians, perhaps indicating a wish to preserve slender Caucasian bloodlines. However, in the following decades, sentiment appeared to shift, with more Eurasian marriages to local Chinese, Melaka Portuguese, and Indians. On the other hand, marriages with Europeans had the social and political advantage of association with the prestige of the colonial masters. These marriages were easily accepted by all lower-status communities. However, it is important to note that such marriages were relatively uncommon at that time. Illicit unions between European men and local women, and even enforced or enslaved/bonded relationships, were more common, starting off with the Portuguese invasion of Melaka in 1511. In the following centuries, this tradition was carried on by others, with many Europeans preferring one or more Asian women at their sexual disposal rather than marrying them. The number of Indian marriages was negligible in comparison with those among Catholics of other races. Large-scale Indian migration was still several decades away, with the opening of the rubber industry in the late nineteenth–early twentieth centuries.[57] The first recorded 'Chindian' (Chinese-Indian) marriage took place at Bukit Timah's St Joseph's Church. Antoni Goon Ah Khit and Malacca-born Angelica David (daughter of David) were married on the 10th January 1870.

## The Life of Pedro Tan Nong Keah (1808–c.1886)

No accurate accounts of the life of an early Catholic convert exist to date. Information has either been lost or has never been properly recorded. Today, 200 years on, almost all information has been lost. However, many aspects of Tan Nong Keah's early life are not specific to himself or even his compatriots.[58] His story mirrors the modern narrative of Singapore, a melting-pot of cultures, ideas, opportunities, and pitfalls. No pictures or images of Tan have survived. For someone like him, conversion to another religion may have seemed tantamount to rejection of part of his Chinese cultural identity.[59] In essence, old Singapore was a place where one could reinvent oneself. While Singapore was a cultural melting-pot, there is little evidence demonstrating active, consistent, and close social relationships among the different groups. Tan's story is a bitter-sweet narrative which provides us with a rare glimpse into this previously hidden world, a precursor to our own time.

Little is known of Tan Nong Keah's activities prior to his contact with the Catholic missionary priest, China-born Father John Tschu, who introduced Tan to the Catholic faith in 1839. Father Tschu claimed in late 1839 that he had recruited a 'wealthy merchant'. This merchant was not identified, but coincidentally, church baptism records show Tan Nong Keah's conversion to the Roman Catholic faith in late December 1839.[60]

The original information about Tan was retrieved from his great-grandson in 1981, and although the information was not complete, the author has managed to fill in parts of the Tan's story in order to provide an accurate and personalised account. Tan was born in the Teochew-speaking region of China's Guangdong province, in 1808. It was claimed he was not originally a Tan but had been adopted into the wealthy Tan clan in China. It is not known when he arrived in Singapore. However, December 1839 saw Tan baptised into the Catholic church. In the baptism registers, Tan was baptised Pedro (or Peter) 'Ano-Kigna', at the age of thirty-one. The presiding priest, Father Jean-Marie Beurel (1812–1872), transcribed his name as a phonetic rendering of the spoken words, 'Nong Keah'. Tan was not the first person of Chinese descent to be admitted into the church. Several of his fellow countrymen had already done the same, starting from around 1834.

The adoption of 'Pedro', Tan's new Christian name, is unusual. The use of an Iberian variation of 'Peter' appears to indicate the social proximity Pedro and other China-born men had with the large Melaka Portuguese congregation. Pedro's brother also adopted the name 'Joao', which is the Portuguese variation of 'John'. Another parishioner adopted a popular Portuguese name 'Joachim' (1841) – and in 1850, there is a reference in the marriage registers to a China-born Chinese man calling himself 'Peter de Santa Maria', with no reference to any Chinese or clan name at all.[61]

In many cases Tan's Chinese clan name was dropped and only his first names used: 'Nong Keah', along with his Christian name, 'Pedro'. Consequently, he was often recorded simply as Pedro 'No Kea' (or A'No Kia, Neo Kea, Noh Kia, Nokea, Nokiah, Anokia, or Anokian). Among the Catholic Teochew community of the 1830s, this seems to have been a common practice, and one that lasted well into the 1850s and even 1860s. Most China-born men dropped their clan names, often simply using their adopted Christian name coupled with their Chinese first names – in Nong Keah's case, 'Pedro No Kea'. His immediate family members used No Kea as a surname, and carried this practice on well into the 1870s. This might indicate an unwillingness to associate themselves with the old traditional *kongsi* or clan organisations. Chinese clans controlled Chinese social, economic and political structures, and in the Southeast Asian region, they also acted as a brotherhood organisation within an overarching economic partnership.⁶² Elements that bound *kongsi* members together and to the brotherhood included their shared clan-names or surnames. If de-emphasising their traditional clan names was a way of dissociating themselves from their traditional *kongsi*, why was this necessary? Unfortunately, no reference is made to this issue in the church correspondence or literature of the day. Nevertheless, there was clear animosity between traditional *kongsi* and new converts. Historians mention how 'refugees' (as a result of disputes and conflicts with *kongsi*) from *kongsi* in Singapore were known to move to areas outside and beyond *kongsi* control.⁶³ The converts' lack of an overarching *kongsi* did not necessarily mean that they viewed or used their Catholic parishes as a new kind of *kongsi*, but as in their former *kongsi*, these converts fostered a strong sense of brotherhood within their church.⁶⁴

On 6 September 1841, Tan married Joanna An Gau. Little is revealed about her background in church records. Her parents were Catholic, and still alive at the time of the marriage. Judging by her surname, and according to family sources, she was of *Orang Asli* or indigenous descent. The couple had one child, a girl named Victoria.⁶⁵ Joanna died young on 5 May 1847. On-going research appears to show Tan may have concurrently had two other 'wives', which was unconventional for a practitioner of the Roman Catholic faith. By 1848, he had three children, Victoria, Maria and John.⁶⁶

Tan's business interests grew: he had large plantation landholdings in Bukit Timah, ran a business from Boat Quay (Kea & Co, Chop Ban Seng), and by the mid-1840s had gained a *surat sungei* (a permit to develop river-bank plantations). He became the *Kangchu* (headman) of the Sungei Benut river-bank settlement in Johore, the southernmost region of the Malayan peninsula.⁶⁷ He ran gambier and pepper plantations, although family sources claim he also dealt in opium (which was a common enough crop at the time).⁶⁸ This point is clarified by French historian Eric Guerassimoff, who wrote of Tan's disappointment at Roman Catholic priest Father Augustine Périé's unwillingness to let him supplement his income with opium cultivation.⁶⁹

In 1851, disaster struck the Catholic community. Local Teochew groups and *kongsi* began attacking Catholic Teochew properties from early 1851. Many plantations were attacked and after five days of rioting, the press reported 500 dead (disputable) and about twenty-eight plantations destroyed. Riots were a relatively common occurrence at the time. There were three riots between 1846 and 1854: the Chinese Funeral Riots in 1846, the Anti-Catholic Riots in 1851, and the Hokkien-Teochew Riots in 1854. Circumstances leading up to the Anti-Catholic Riots were two-fold. By the 1840s, arable land in Singapore was getting scarce. Competition for plantations was so heavy that by 1845, many began moving into Johore to look for greener pastures.[70] Tensions began to build when local *kongsi* members claimed British colonial administrators favoured Christian converts and rumours had it that rich Christian planters were dealing in opium, therefore circumventing *kongsi* control.[71]

Tan had sustained attacks on his properties months before the riots began. In late September or early October 1850, suspicious fires destroyed property on his rural plantation.[72] Several months later, during the Anti-Catholic Riots, he was pushed out of his Bukit Timah plantation and forced to sneak back inside with the help of a local policeman. In 1886, the Straits Times recounted:

> *Pedro Neo Keah wanted to go to Bukit Timah to his gambier and pepper plantations, and Mr Henry Kraal managed to take him up and down, having bagged poor Pedro in a gunny bag and stowed him at the bottom of the hack. He had three ponies on the road rattling away at breakneck pace.*
>
> Source: Notes from the Kampong. *The Singapore Free Press and Mercantile Advertiser*, 17 July 1886, p. 36.

Tan and his three children, Victoria, Maria and John, survived. He eventually settled down with his third wife, Anna Lim Ah Keow and had five more children.

Tan's fortunes continued despite this personal setback in 1851. Within three years in 1854, Tan owned a 1,000-acre tapioca plantation in Serangoon (Trafalgar estate), gambier and pepper plantations at Bukit Timah and in the Upper Toa Payoh area, and had a share in at least fifteen farms in the Pontian, Ayer Hitam (Air Hitam) and Pinggan areas of Johore by the 1860s.⁷³ Around this time, the Catholic church was beginning to participate in Tan's business ventures. As early as July 1848, Father Jean-Marie Beurel, referred to co-owning a 17,000-tree nutmeg plantation with a 'Christian Chinese', to raise funds for church expenses, although no mention of Tan was made.⁷⁴ In the meantime, the church was arguably reliant on merchants like Tan to help fund church projects, especially for new buildings.⁷⁵ Fundraising was always a challenge for the church, but philanthropists like Tan were certainly not the only contributors; contributions were solicited from all parts of Singapore society, both Catholic and non-Catholic. However, as a long-term parishioner, Tan would have been relied on as a benefactor on numerous occasions, and also for potential business opportunities. In 1863, with church approval, Father Augustine Périé (1832–1892), secured key financial support from Tan and leased an area in Pontian Kechil (Kecil), Johore, about seventy-five kilometres north-west of Singapore.⁷⁶ He was allowed to grow only pepper and gambier. However, Father Périé underestimated the high costs of running such a venture, and was unwilling to supplement his profits by growing opium, as most other planters did, much to Tan's disappointment. When Périé's venture began to fail, Tan, his primary financier, decided to abandon the investment. The Pontian Kechil venture was vacated and Tan took it over, along with another one in Ayer Hitam. Several years later he took control of neighbouring Pinggan as well. It seems there was little compensation for the Roman Catholic church's losses.⁷⁷

Further clashes with the local *kongsi* occurred around October 1864 when St Joseph's Church (Bukit Timah) parish priest Father Issaly took a young girl out of a *kongsi*-owned brothel and had her placed in the CHIJ orphanage. This event caused such a stir that Tan and his family, as Catholics and known associates of Issaly, were temporarily forced to flee to Macao, leaving their plantation at Pontian Kechil.⁷⁸

Despite Tan's status as a Roman Catholic and clan outsider in the 1840s, 1850s and 1860s, he appeared to have redeemed himself in the eyes of his *kongsi* compatriots by the late 1860s. He was one of eighty Singapore Chinese merchants who were signatories to a scroll presented to the visiting British Duke of Edinburgh in November 1869.⁷⁹ In 1874, he headed an official delegation to the British colonial Governor of Singapore, representing 299 Singapore gambier and pepper merchants voicing their collective business concerns to government.[80] Around that time Tan was running his business Chop Kiam Seng from 48 Boat Quay.

Despite Tan's rise to respectability in the 1860s and 1870s, he was still implicated in at least one reprehensible incident. In 1876, Tan was one of a group of wealthy merchants who held a monopoly on remittance payments to China. In December 1876, the British colonial government decided to open its first official Post Office in Singapore. Fearful they would lose their monopoly, Tan and his merchant compatriots began circulating posters in the city making false and incendiary claims against the new Post Office. A violent riot ensued (now referred to as the Post Office Riots) and three people were killed, with several more injured. Several days later a *Singapore Daily Times* article (19 December 1876) claimed Tan and six other wealthy merchants 'in their youth' had not walked 'in the path of righteousness' and in pursuit of 'flourishing and wealthy business' had 'ruined trades and taken away life'.[81]

Towards the last two decades of Tan's life, he travelled with his family. In April 1873, he journeyed to Hong Kong with his wife Anna Lim and his five children, seven grandchildren and seven servants. It is unclear how individual members of the family connected to each other. To date there is little evidence on whether his children from other wives tied in with his new family or the family business. His eldest son John Tan Hay Seng (born c.1848), ran a shipping business and owned several vessels which operated around the Singapore harbour in the early 1890s. However, technical mishaps, accidents and an unsuccessful synthetic dye venture may have brought about his financial downfall in later years.[82] Owing to these mishaps and also exclusion from his father's will, John Tan died a poor man in 1902.[83] He reportedly was a mentee of SJI founder Father Jean-Marie Beurel and was one of the original students of that school when it first opened in 1852.[84] Tan's daughter Victoria Tan Choo Lan married Paul Ng Ah Soi, a China-born rice merchant she had met at catechism classes while a young girl. Victoria died in 1910 at her home at 3 Tank Road.[85]

Pedro Tan Nong Keah himself died around 1886. His will must have been disputed because it took almost a decade before the settlement was completed.[86] Strangely, no one apart from his son (from his later marriage), John Baptist Tan, and his second wife Anna Lim was named as a beneficiary. Nevertheless, Tan's greatest legacy was his philanthropy in supporting the Catholic church. He was probably the original large-scale parishioner philanthropist, a role that would grow in importance from the 1880s. Although his contributions would be dwarfed by others in the latter half of the nineteenth century, it was Tan who set the ball rolling. His familiarity with business, and the church's willingness to participate in profit-making ventures continued into the 1870s, when the church funded a young China-born parishioner, Jacobe Low Khiok Chiang (1843–1911), to start up a mercantile business, Kiam Hoa Heng, in Bangkok and Singapore. The Tan family would link up (via marriage) with these new entrepreneurial family networks in the following decades, and Tan's own grandson, David Wee Cheng Soon (1875–1944) would go on to be one of a handful of major Catholic church philanthropists from the 1900s until his death in 1944.

## References/Notes

[1] Buckley, C.B. (1902/1984). *An Anecdotal History of Old Times in Singapore 1819–1867*. p. 242.

[2] Good Shepherd Church. Baptism Register 1832–1867. SING 0001, #1, National Archives of Singapore.

[3] Good Shepherd Church. Baptism Register. *Ibid*; Good Shepherd Church, Liber Matrimoniorum 1833–1857. SING 0001, #3, National Archives of Singapore; Rerceretnam, M. (2020). Intermarriage, religious conversions, and new Peranakans within multi-ethnic communities in colonial Singapore: The development of early multi-ethnic Roman Catholic communities, c. 1830s to 1860. In *Chapters on Asia* (2019). Singapore: National Library Board.

[4] Desai, D. R. Sar. (1968), 'The Portuguese Administration in Malacca, 15-11-1641', in *International Conference on Asian History, 5th-10th August 1968*, Dept of History, University of Malaya, pp. 1-3, 4. https://myrepositori.pnm.gov.my/xmlui/bitstream/handle/1/605/JB0093_PAMa.pdf?sequence=1&isAllowed=y accessed on 13 July 2021.

[5] Buckley,C.B. (1902/1984). *An Anecdotal History of Old Times in Singapore 1819–1867*, p. 245.

[6] Guerassimoff, E. (1997). The gangzhu of Johor: Memories of a French missionary in Malaysia, 1859–1870. In *Études Chinoises*, Vol. XVI, No. 1, 1997. p. 107.

7   Buckley, C.B. (1902/1984). *An Anecdotal History of Old Times in Singapore 1819-1867.* p. 245.
8   Buckley, C.B. *Ibid.* pp. 242–45. 8
9   Annals of the Propagation of the Faith, Vol. XLII, 10 September 1833.
10  Good Shepherd Church. Baptism Register 1832–1867. See entry dated 18 August 1833.
11  Interview with Mr Low Yeow Teng (1938–), 2 December 2019, Shantou, China. Interviewed by Marc Rerceretnam.
12  Information from Paul Theseira, 4 July 2021.
13  Chia, T.Y, Dr Peter. (1985). *Memoir of a Straits Born Baba.* Unpublished, personal collection; Rerceretnam, M. Descendants of the Low family and the Khiam Hoa Heng family enterprises. Facebook (private page).
14  Trocki, CA. (1979/2007). *Prince of Pirates: The Temenggongs and the Development of Johor and Singapore 1784–1885.* Singapore: NUS Press. p. 110.
15  Anonymous. (1836). *The Sessions. The Singapore Free Press and Mercantile Advertiser,* 12 May 1836. p. 3. Microfilm Reel NL1555, NewspaperSG http://eresources.nlb.gov.sg/newspapers/Digitised/Article/singfreepressa18360512-1.2.19
16  Rerceretnam, M. (2020). Intermarriage, religious conversions and new Peranakans within multi-ethnic communities in colonial Singapore. In *Chapters on Asia: Selected Papers from the Lee Kong Chian Research Fellowship* (2019), (2020). Singapore: National Library Board.
17  Braga-Blake, M., Ebert-Oehlers, A. & Pereira A.A. (2017). *Singapore Eurasians: Memories, Hopes and Dreams.* Singapore: World Scientific Publishing. p. 33.
18  Rerceretnam, M. (2011). *Black Europeans, the Indian Coolies and Empire: Colonialisation and Christianized Indians in colonial Malaya and Singapore, c. 1870s–c. 1950s.* Saarbrücken, Germany: VDM Verlag Dr Müller. pp. 48–49.
19  Pilon, M. & Weiler, D. (2011). *The French in Singapore: An Illustrated History (1819–today).* Singapore: Didier Millet). p. 44.
20  Good Shepherd Church. Baptism Register 1832–1867.
21  Ackerman, S. & Lee, R. (1988). *Heaven in Transition.* Honolulu: University of Hawaii Press. pp. 29, 38; Loh, K.A. (1963). *Fifty years of the Anglican Church in Singapore Island 1909–1959.* Singapore: University of Singapore. p. 5. Protestant missionary groups like the London Missionary Society (LMS), who were established in Singapore years before the French Roman Catholic missions, left Singapore for China in 1846.
22  Malayan Christian Council, Minutes. Summary Record of Hearing held in the Conference Room at 11am on Thursday, 23rd August, 1956. In Karim's Blog, https://akarimomar.files.wordpress.com/2014/06/malayanchristiancouncil-constitutionhearing-aug1956-frame.jpg accessed 14 February 2020.
23  Loh, K.A. (1963). *Fifty years of the Anglican Church in Singapore Island 1909–1959.* p. 5.
24  Panikkar, K.M. (1953). *Asia and Western Dominance: A Survey of the Vasco da Gama Epoch of Asian History.* London: George Allen and Unwin). pp. 445, 447; James, G. D. (1962). *Missionary Tours in Malaya,* Singapore: Malaya Evangelistic Fellowship. pp. 36, 40–1; *Straits Settlements Annual Report 1935.* Singapore: Government Printing Office, 1936. pp. 803–10.

25  James, G.D. (1962). *Missionary Tours in Malaya*. p. 40. It was also noted that such assertions by Christian missionaries were commonly followed by a 'hot argument'.
26  Daniel, J.R. (1992). *Indian Christians in Peninsular Malaysia*. Kuala Lumpur: Tamil Annual Conference, 1992, p. 47. The states where Indian Christians predominated were also the same states where Indian labour was actively recruited for Malaya; Sandhu, K. S. (1969). *Indians in Malaya: Some Aspects of their Immigration and Settlement 1786-1957*. Cambridge: Cambridge University Press. p. 82; Arasaratnam, S. (1970). *Indians in Malaysia and Singapore*. London: Oxford University Press. p. 15; Khoo, B. L. (1972). This church is a replica of the one at Lourdes. *New Nation*. Singapore, 14 April 1972. At the Church of Our Lady of Lourdes church in Singapore, the article claims most of the congregation was made up of 'merchants' and clerks, with a smaller proportion of labourers.
27  Interview with Mr Gabriel Lourdes (born 1925), Singapore, 1 September 1997. Interviewed by Marc Rerceretnam; Cook, J.A. Bethune. (1907). *Sunny Singapore: An Account of the Place and its People with a Sketch of the Results of Missionary Work*. London: Elliot Stock. pp. 134–5; Caplan, L. (1980). Caste and Castelessness among South Indian Christians. In *Contributions to Indian Sociology*, 1980, 14 (2). p. 221.
28  Marriages: St John's Cathedral. Kuala Lumpur, 6 April 1891–29 January 1906; Marriages: St Anthony's Church. Kuala Lumpur, 2 April 1923–28 January 1950.
29  Baptisms: Church of Our Lady of Lourdes, Singapore, 14 May 1884–15 September 1895.
30  James, G.D. (1962). *Missionary Tours in Malaya*. p. 30.
31  James, G.D. (1962). *Ibid*. pp. 36–37.
32  Interview with Mr James Sebastian, (1933-2020). Sydney, January 1999. Interviewed by Marc Rerceretnam.
33  Rerceretnam, M. (2011). *Black Europeans, the Indian Coolies and Empire: Colonialisation and Christianized Indians in colonial Malaya and Singapore, c. 1870s–c. 1950s*. pp. 299–303.
34  Good Shepherd Church. Baptism Register 1832–1867; Good Shepherd Church. Liber Matrimoniorum 1833–1857. SING 0001, #3, National Archives of Singapore.
35  Bayly, S. (1989). *Saints, Goddesses and Kings*. Cambridge: Cambridge University Press. p. 19.
36  Braga-Blake, M. & Ebert-Oehlers, A. (1992). *Eurasians in Singapore: Memories and Hopes*. Singapore: Times Editions. p. 23. An element of shame about their status as 'non-Europeans' fed this trend. Similar shame associated with being non-white was strong among other English-educated, middle-class Asian communities.
37  Pereira, A.A. (1991–1992). *Ethnic Adaptations of Religious Orthodoxy: A study of Chinese, Indian and Eurasian Catholics in Singapore*. Singapore: University of Singapore (Academic Exercise). p. 40.
38  Baptisms: Church of Our Lady of Lourdes, 14 May 1884–15 September 1895, Singapore; Marriage Book: Church of Our Lady of Lourdes, 7 May 1884–7 April 1947, Singapore; Marriages: St John's Cathedral, 6.4.1891–29.1.1906, Kuala Lumpur.

39 Interview with David Sebastian, (born 1931). Singapore, 9 August 1996. Interviewed by Marc Rerceretnam.
40 Pereira, A.A. (1991–1992). *Ethnic Adaptations of Religious Orthodoxy*, p. 40.
41 Bugge, H. (1994). *Mission and Tamil Society*. Surrey, UK: Curzon Press. p. 140; Bayly, S. (1989). *Saints, Goddesses and Kings*. pp. 381–383. St Francis Xavier, St James the Great (d. 44 CE) and the Virgin Mary were popular adopted objects of worship from as early as 1644; Farmer, D.H. (1992). *The Oxford Dictionary of Saint*. Oxford: Oxford University Press, 1992 (1978).
42 Daniel, J.R. (1992). *Indian Christians in Peninsular Malaysia*. Kuala Lumpur: Tamil Annual Conference, 1992. p. 157.
43 Bugge, H. (1994). *Mission and Tamil Society*. p. 43. Thurston, E. (1909). *Caste and Tribes of Southern India*, Vol. 6. Madras: Government Press, 1909. p. 428.
44 Many of these names were also used by Goan immigrants. Goa was formerly a Portuguese protectorate. Goans made up only a small proportion of the South Indian population of Malaya and Singapore.
45 Civil Establishment Listings. Straits Settlements Blue Books (annual), 1871–1946.
46 Pereira, A.A. (1991–1992). *Ethnic Adaptations of Religious Orthodoxy*. p. 40.
47 Good Shepherd Church. Baptism Register 1832–1867; Good Shepherd Church. Liber Matrimoniorum 1833–1857. SING 0001, #3, National Archives of Singapore.
48 Sarkissian, M. (2005). Being Portuguese in Malacca: The Politics of Folk Culture in Malaysia. In *Etnografica*, Vol. IX, No. 1, p. 152.
49 Rerceretnam, M. (2012). Intermarriage in colonial Malaya and Singapore: A case study of nineteenth- and early twentieth-century Roman Catholic and Methodist Asian communities. In *The Journal of Southeast Asian Studies*, Vol. 43, No. 2, June 2012. p. 318.
50 Rerceretnam, M. (2020). Intermarriage, religious conversions and new Peranakans within multi-ethnic communities in colonial Singapore. In *Chapters on Asia* (pending publication). Singapore: National Library Board.
51 Song, O.S. (1923/2016). *One Hundred Years' History of the Chinese in Singapore*. Singapore: National Library Board. p. 712.
52 Rudolph, J. (1998). *Reconstructing Identities: A Social History of the Babas in Singapore*. Aldershot, UK: Ashgate. p. 30.
53 Not included in this number are a few first generation European-Asian, Eurasian-Asian and other variations. However, for the purposes of discussing family groups who would later become part of the wider Singapore Peranakan community, I have excluded these marriages for the time being.
54 Good Shepherd Church. Liber Matrimoniorum 1833–1857. SING 0001, #3, National Archives of Singapore.
55 Li, M. From 'Sons the Yellow Emperor' to 'Children of Indonesian Soil': Studying Peranakan Chinese based on the Batavia Kong Koan Archives. In *The Journal of Southeast Asian Studies*, Vol, 34, No. 2, June 2003. p. 215.
56 Rerceretnam, M. (2020). Intermarriage, religious conversions and new Peranakans within multi-ethnic communities in colonial Singapore.
57 Rerceretnam, M. *Ibid.*.

58 Interview with Mr Philip Wee Peng Leng (1904–1991). Interviewed by Marjorie and Phyllis Wee on 18 August 1981. Personal collection. Mr Wee was the great grandson of Pedro Tan Nong Keah (1808–c.1886).
59 Andaya, B. Watson. (2015). Come Home, Come Home! Chineseness, John Sung and Theatrical Evangelism in 1930s Southeast Asia. In *Southeast Asian Studies at Freiburg*. University of Freiburg, Occasional Paper No. 23, February 2015. p. 1.
60 Good Shepherd Church. Baptism Register 1832–1867.
61 Good Shepherd Church. *Ibid*.
62 Trocki, C.A. (1990). *Opium and Empire: Chinese Society in Colonial Singapore, 1800–1910*. New York: Cornell University Press. pp. 3–4, 11.
63 Trocki, C.A. *Ibid*. p. 101.
64 Trocki, C.A. *Ibid*. p. 108.
65 Good Shepherd Church. Baptism Register 1832–1867.
66 Information supplied by Juliana Lim, 25 April 2021.
67 Buckley, C.B. (1902/1984) *An Anecdotal History of Old Times in Singapore, 1819–1867*. Singapore: Oxford University Press. p. 431; Trocki, C.A. (2007). Prince of Pirates: The Temenggongs and the Development of Johor and Singapore. Singapore: NUS Press. pp. 218–222, 117, 119; The Colonial Directory of the Straits Settlements, including Sarawak, Labuan, Bangkok and Saigon. (1873). Singapore: Mission Press. Microfilm no. NL2362, p. 19B.
68 Interview with Mr Philip Wee Peng Leng (1904–1991). Interviewed by Marjorie and Phyllis Wee on 18 August 1981. Personal collection.
69 Guerassimoff, E. (1997).The gangzhu of Johor: Memories of a French missionary in Malaysia, 1859–1870. In *Études Chinoises*, Vol. XVI, No. 1, 1997. pp. 124–125.
70 Wilfred Blythe. (1969). *The Impact of Chinese Secret Societies in Malaya*. Suffolk, UK: Oxford University Press. pp. 70–71; Buckley, C.B. (1902/1984). *An Anecdotal History of Old Times in Singapore, 1819–1867*. p. 431; Guerassimoff, E. (1997). The gangzhu of Johor: Memories of a French missionary in Malaysia. In *Études Chinoises*, Vol. XVI, No. 1, 1997. p. 113.
71 Trocki, C.A. (1990). *Opium and Empire: Chinese Society in Colonial Singapore, 1800–1910*. New York: Cornell University Press. pp. 108–9. Trocki does not appear to be aware that Pedro Tan Nong Keah did deal in opium; Interview with Mr Philip Wee Peng Leng (1904–1991). Interviewed by Marjorie and Phyllis Wee on 18 August 1981. Personal collection; Guerassimoff, E. (1997).The gangzhu of Johor: Memories of a French missionary in Malaysia. p. 124.
72 Anonymous, 'Local'. *The Singapore Free Press and Mercantile Advertiser*, 4 October 1850. p. 2. Microfilm Reel NL1589, NewspaperSG http://eresources.nlb.gov.sg/newspapers/Digitised/Article/singfreepressa18501004-1.2.3
73 This is possibly Mukim 17, under Grants 2 (Survey no. 1054) and 12 (Survey no. 1064). Mukim 17 Lot 30, Grant 12 was acquired by the Land Office in 1923 to form part of a Rifle Range; Guerassimoff, E. The gangzhu of Johor: Memories of a French missionary in Malaysia, 1859–1870. In *Études Chinoises*, Vol. XVI, No. 1, 1997. pp. 122, 137.

74 Beurel, J.M. (1848). Letter addressed to Mr Albrand, dated 28 July 1848. In J. M. Beurel, *The Letters of Fr. J. M. Beurel relating to the establishment of St. Joseph's Institution Singapore*. (Unpublished). p. 17. Translated, edited and with a monograph by Rev. Brother Anthony, St. Xavier's Institution, Penang. Singapore: St Joseph's Institution Archives.

75 Anonymous. (1887). Picturesque and Busy Singapore. *Straits Times Weekly Issue*, 14 March 1887. NewspaperSG; Buckley, C.B. (1902/1984). *An Anecdotal History of Old Times in Singapore*. pp. 253, 254; Guerassimoff, E. (1997). The gangzhu of Johor: Memories of a French missionary in Malaysia. In *Études Chinoises*, Vol. XVI, No. 1, 1997. p. 122; Song O.S. (2016/1923) One Hundred Years' History of the Chinese in Singapore. Singapore: National Library Board. p. 47.

76 Guerassimoff, E. *Ibid*. p. 115.

77 Guerassimoff, E. *Ibid*. pp. 128, 137.

78 Liew, C. (2016). *Persecution of Chinese Christians in Early Colonial Singapore 1845–1869*. Historical Inquiry Report, Roman Catholic Archdiocese of Singapore, (unpublished). p. 69.

79 Address to Alfred, Duke of Edinburgh by the Singapore Chinese merchants on the occasion of his visit to Singapore in 1869. [Image of Photograph]. Singapore: National Library. Retrieved from NLB eResources website: http://eresources.nlb.gov.sg/printheritage/detail/920ecc56-9df8-409e-b3ec-f742a6895eea.aspx

80 Anonymous, Advertisements. Straits Observer, 3 December 1874, p. 4. NewspapersSG, http://eresources.nlb.gov.sg/newspapers/Digitised/Article/straitsobserver18741203-1.2.9.1, accessed on 6 April 2019.

81 Yong, C.Y. (2016). Chinese Post Office Riots. Singapore: Infopedia, 2016, National Library Board. https://eresources.nlb.gov.sg/infopedia/articles/SIP_1004_2011-07-15.html, accessed on 1 May 2019. Tan's accomplices were Tan Seng Poh, Tay Lee Soon, Khaw Ohong Nghee, Low How Lim, Goh Yow and Kang Ah Peah; Guerassimoff, E. (1997). The gangzhu of Johor: Memories of a French missionary in Malaysia. In *Études Chinoises*, Vol. XVI, No. 1, 1997. p. 136. (See endnote 117).

82 Anonymous. A Trial Trip. *Daily Advertiser*, 31 March 1891. p. 2, NewspaperSG, http://eresources.nlb.gov.sg/newspapers/Digitised/Article/dailyadvertiser18910331-1.2.4, accessed on 12 April 2019.

83 Anonymous. Death of Mr. Tan Hay Seng. *The Straits Times*, 2 December 1902. p. 5, NewspaperSG http://eresources.nlb.gov.sg/newspapers/Digitised/Article/straitstimes19021202-1.2.38 , accessed on 10 October 2018.

84 Buckley, C.B. (1902/1984). *An Anecdotal History of Old Times in Singapore 1819–1867*. p. 270.

85 Interview with Mr Philip Wee Peng Leng (1904–1991). Interviewed by Marjorie and Phyllis Wee on 18 August 1981. Personal collection; Baptismregister, Church of Sts Peter & Paul, 28 January 1868.

86 Anonymous. Advertisements, *The Straits Times*, 30 May1898. p. 3, NewspaperSG http://eresources.nlb.gov.sg/newspapers/Digitised/Article/straitstimes18980530-1.2.54.1 accessed on 23 March 2018.

Chapter 3

# Clans and *Kongsi*

Traditional clan organisations in southern China played a key role in everyday life. The clan or *kongsi* (公司), was a social organisation for people of common descent. In Singapore, overseas migrants used these organisations to overcome economic difficulties and ostracism. The *kongsi* were originally set up as benevolent entities providing mutual assistance and bonding. Their primary aim was to take care of members who became sick or unemployed. They were clan-based and geographically specific, and all new arrivals from China effectively were obliged to join one. The concept of 'clan' was based on the idea of kinship among individuals of the same surname, coming from the same village or from several nearby villages in the same area. In later decades, this idea was expanded to include not only sharing the same surname from the same geographical locality but also sharing the same dialect.[1] The earliest clan organisation in Singapore was set up by the Cantonese in 1822. Despite the Teochews being the dominant dialect group on the island at the time, they officially set up their own Ngee Ann Kongsi as late as 1845. This was largely because the Teochew population had always been scattered throughout the island, many involved in the agricultural sector, outside of the city precinct, unlike other dialect groups.[2] As time went on, in tandem with increasingly lucrative economic opportunities in Singapore, the *kongsi* expanded beyond simply looking after the welfare of their members. Many got heavily involved in the operation and control of labour and businesses, and in the worst-case scenario, in gambling, opium dens and prostitution. In time, they even posed a significant threat to law and order in Singapore.[3]

Even in their early days, clans controlled most aspects of everyday Chinese life in Singapore. They controlled the temples, and organised labour and businesses, in conjunction with local *towkays* (business bosses). As a clansman, it was almost impossible to get anything done outside of the clan. In these early days, a clan organisation and a secret society were often one and the same. Both organisations identified with a specific community group, provided welfare services, and played a critical role in organising and financing business and labour. While Teochew clan organisations officially started only from 1845, there is evidence that such organisations were in existence by 1833, when new converts and Catholic clergy were directly threatened by their agents.[4]

## Teochew clan conflict with the Catholics

By the 1830s, merchants like Tan Nong Keah were doing well in Singapore. Tan's connections with and financial backing from his wealthy adopted Tan family meant that he had entered the island market riding high. He owned large tracts of land in the north of the island, and like many of his Teochew *towkay* compatriots, he specialised in gambier, pepper and opium.[5] The gambier plant is well known as a favoured companion to the areca nut (from the Areca palm) which traditionally has been wrapped in betel leaves for chewing, with stimulant, addictive and toxic effects similar to those experienced by tobacco chewers and smokers. However, more importantly in economic terms, gambier was greatly in demand as a tanning and dyeing agent for mass-produced materials in the west.[6] Pepper too was a condiment staple, worldwide. Opium was all too popular a crop, offering high profits, but it was troublesome to cultivate due to the need for an expensive government licence to legally produce and sell it. However, despite the hazards of illegal opium production, temptation often overcame farmers in those days.[7]

By the late 1830s or early 1840s, Tan Nong Keah owned the Trafalgar Estate located at the seventh milestone on Upper Serangoon Road, near present day Hougang.[8] This was a sprawling 1,000-acre plantation (approximately four square kilometres). He also had a city-based business at Boat Quay, where he stored and readied his products for shipment to overseas markets.[9] Like other successful merchants, he worked through existing social, economic, and political structures to ensure all went to plan. This would have included cooperating with his local clan and its network.

In late December 1839, Tan Nong Keah renounced his Taoist beliefs, was baptised as a Roman Catholic, and left his clan.[10] He adopted the Christian name 'Pedro'. For several months prior to his conversion, recent arrival Father John Tschu, a Catholic priest, had met Pedro at his Boat Quay business and found to his own surprise that he was amenable to listening to his evangelical message. Although there had been conversions prior to December 1839, this one was different. This new convert, Tan, was 'wealthy', a point emphasised in the church records of the time. The conversion of a Teochew clansman, especially a wealthy one, was not taken lightly by the Teochew clan organisation. After the conversion of the first four Teochew men in 1833, Father Étienne Albrand had been threatened, and similarly the clans targeted Teochew converts, threatening to cut off their queues/pigtails (辮子) and tear off their Chinese clothes. As Father Albrand observed in 1833:

> *They were very angry when the first four of their members became Christians. Luckily, these four Christians are strong in their faith. But every day, they have to struggle against the heads of the Secret Societies to which they had belonged, whom they called, 'head of the devil'. One day, they threatened them, to spoil their names in China, to tear away their pig-tails and to take away their Chinese clothing.*
>
> Source: Annals of the Propagation of the Faith, XLII, 10 Sept 1833.

Fortunately, these threats did not eventuate. Nevertheless, it was clear the local clan was not happy about the church's intrusion into what it deemed to be its territory. By the early 1840s, the number of Teochew converts had grown considerably, and the new Teochew church St Joseph's was established at rural Kranji in 1846. It was moved a few years later to its current site at Bukit Timah.[11] The French Mission clergy appeared to take a proactive stance, often aggressively advocating for their parishioners. In one event around December 1863, Father Issaly was approached by a Chinese parishioner from the Portuguese Mission church. His daughter had been kidnapped by the local clan and forced into prostitution at a local teahouse. He had approached the Portuguese Mission priest, who had refused to help him. Father Issaly firstly sent a letter of warning to the teahouse owner, but after this was ignored, he got a young man to covertly rescue the girl and take her to the safety of the CHIJ orphanage. This action angered the clan and serious threats were made. As a prominent Catholic parishioner, Pedro Tan Nong Keah was forced to flee his plantation properties in 1864, even though he had no apparent link to the rescue.[12]

Crime was rife in Singapore during the 1800s. British colonial authorities made little attempt to police the rural districts of the island, such as plantation areas, despite the ongoing proliferation of crime in such areas.[13] The crime situation was exacerbated by low gambier prices in the 1840s, causing a related increase in unemployment and criminal activity (close to a third of all Teochews were employed in the gambier industry up to the 1850s).[14] In conjunction with this deteriorating backdrop, membership of traditional clan organisations soared, estimated at between 10,000 and 20,000 in 1846 alone. It would be too much of an assumption to equate every criminal act perpetrated against a Teochew Christian with a clan attack on Christian converts, but existing animosity between clans and converts probably did aggravate crimes and acts of violence when the perpetrators realised that their victims were converts, not clan members. From the late 1840s, attacks on Teochew Catholic persons or property became more and more common, especially from 1849 onward. Most of these crimes occurred in the rural districts of Singapore, and usually involved armed robbery and kidnapping, occasionally with fatal results.[15]

## The Anti-Catholic Riots of 1851

The culmination of larger numbers of Teochews continuing to convert, lower gambier farming profits in the 1840s, higher unemployment, and rising crime rates were only part of the problem. From 1819, the northern interior of Singapore island had been largely ignored by the British colonial government. Many migrant farmers and planters made personal arrangements, staked claims, and established farms in these areas without government authority. Even if land technically belonged to the Crown, these squatter-farmers did not pay rent. In response to this, in 1843, the British colonial government began mapping these areas and introduced rents or sold the land to interested parties. This move was not appreciated by the farmers, who were by this point experiencing the negative impacts of falling gambier prices and profits. Around the same time, space for large plantations began to run out. Unable to get large enough properties to farm on, many Teochew planters and *towkays* moved across the water to Johore, where land was plentiful, and the Johore Sultan was keen to entertain new farming opportunities.

Back on the island of Singapore, all these factors were causing increasing tension. The British colonial government had adopted a system of licences which they sold to the highest bidder. These licences provided holders with a virtual monopoly of the market.[16] Growing opium and producing its by-products without a licence was therefore illegal and theoretically robbed the authentic licence holder of potential income. In 1850, rumours about a Chinese Christian flouting the opium monopoly licences added fuel to fire. Although current research does not identify this 'rich' Christian, the descendants of Pedro Tan Nong Keah say

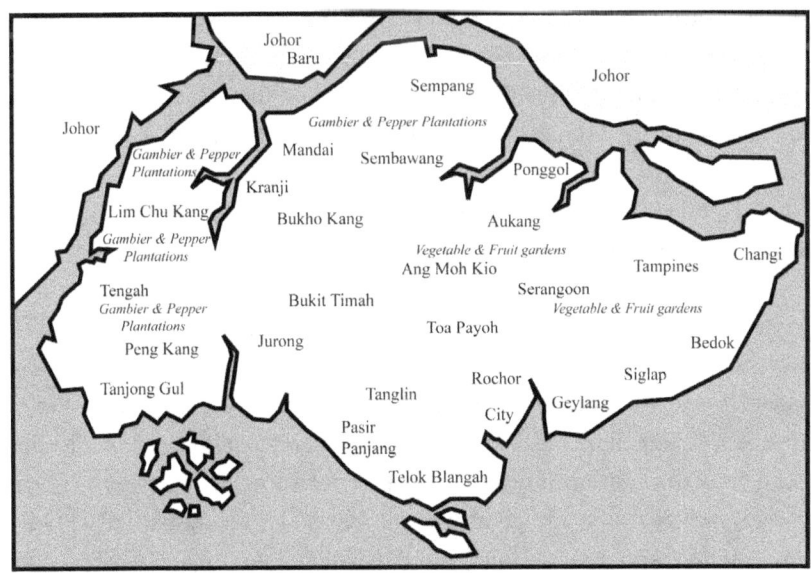

*Singapore in the 1880s*

they are aware he did deal in opium around this time. There is a strong likelihood that the Christian in question was indeed Pedro Tan. In fact, it was as part of an effort to confirm these suspicions that Tan's properties were originally attacked by renegade groups as early as October 1850, a good four months before the violent 'Anti-Catholic Riots' started on 14 February 1851. According to the *Singapore Free Press* newspaper (dated 4 October 1850), the first attack took place in late September and October 1850. Pedro Tan's farm was set alight but only damaged. The property of another Christian, Paul Ah Koon, was destroyed.

Although there were several violent cases involving unprovoked attacks by clan members against Christian Teochews, several incidents in the late 1840s do stand out. According to the *Singapore Free Press* (6 July 1849), the first large-scale incident took place on 25 June 1849. Local clansmen attacked a Teochew Catholic village in rural Singapore, causing 300 villagers to seek refuge in the city. In a separate case, a Teochew Catholic convert, Philip Teo Ho Kah, who had previously identified bandits who robbed his property, was attacked in an apparent act of revenge a few weeks later. Teo was never seen again.

Following Teo's disappearance, a series of criminal prosecutions ensued, with many clan members found guilty, through September 1850 till February 1851. This was followed by the most serious violence yet seen, between 14 and 20 February 1851, when more than 30 plantations owned by Catholic Teochews were attacked. These landholdings and villages were in Serangoon, Bookoo Kang/Bukho Kang (present day Kranji), Bukit Timah, Lauw Choo Kang (present day Mandai), Nam Toh Kang (present day Sembawang), Chan Chu Kang (present day Nee Soon village), and Sungei Benoi.

Groups of twenty to fifty clan members attacked, damaged, and looted whatever they could at the different properties. Even individuals were kidnapped, with large ransoms demanded for their release. Many villagers sought refuge in the city. On 25 February 1851, the colonial Resident Councillor, the Superintendent of Police, and Teochew leader Seah Eu Chin toured the most severely affected areas. The fighting had already subsided by this point and all Christian Teochews had left the rural areas. Seah made a plea for the violence to stop. However, clan leaders had already instructed their members to stop all hostilities shortly before.[17] Contemporary reports from 1851 claim that around 500 people died in the violence, on both sides of the conflict. Investigation of existing church death records has not helped confirm this claimed death toll resulting from the 1851 riots.[18]

There were several outcomes from the 1851 riots. Firstly, compensation for damages was sought by aggrieved Teochew Catholics, via the courts. The clan organisations were forced to pay the sum of $1,500 for damages and losses due to the riots, a figure which many on the Christian side claimed was far too little to properly compensate them. Another outcome likely would have been the reassertion of Teochew Christian resolve and resistance to aggression from clan organisations. Even before the 1851 riots, Teochew Christian groups had a strong sense of fellowship, not dissimilar to that of the Taoist clan compatriots.

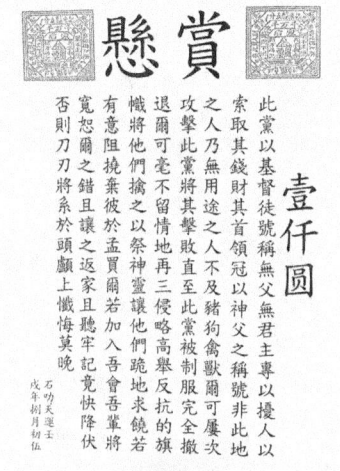

*A reconstruction of an anti-Catholic poster displayed at Ellenborough Markets in 1862.*

Source: Alex Yam.

Violence against the Catholics continued, but in a more muted fashion, and never again at the levels of the 1851 riots. That year was a culmination of a more general resentment and anger that had been swelling since the early 1830s, and was exacerbated by unrelated hostilities against the up-and-coming Hokkien community. The Christians were in the unfortunate position of being in the wrong place at the wrong time. In the immediate years following the riots, tensions remained relatively high but concerted collective action against the community would never take place again. However there were occasional acts of intimidation, or threats. In September 1862, a series of Teochew-language placards were posted at the Ellenborough 'New' Market, a popular place with Teochew Roman Catholic businesses and clientele:

*These people, called Christians, people without a father or a prince, torment the world and men for money. Their chief, to whom is given the title of Father Peré, are creatures born in the world without any useful utility; they are pigs, dogs or other wild animals.*

*That we attack them, we triumph over them, that we come back to the charge we put them in the middle of the road, that we attack them a third time, that we push them without mercy, that we close the standard, we reach finally to make it perfectly master. We take them to sacrifice them and we will see them asking on their knees if these pigs and priest dogs dare to oppose it, we must take them and have them taken to Bombay.*

*If you consent to join us, we will excuse your fault and we will let you go back to your homes. Listen then and remember the good: hurry to make your submission as soon as possible, otherwise the knife is raised on your head, and your repentance will come later.*

Source: Teochew Secret Society Anti-Catholic poster displayed at Ellenborough Markets, September 1862.
*News of the Week, The Straits Times*, 4 October 1862, p. 1.

Nothing came out of this event. For the clan organisations, this level of anger was difficult to sustain. Clan conflict and dialect group differences had begun to dissipate by the 1870s. The Chinese Ching (Qing) dynasty government established a consulate in Singapore by 1877 and the British colonial government set up the Chinese Protectorate around the same time. Both institutions advocated for a united Chinese community, an idea which did not encourage the recognition of clan or dialect differences. This conciliatory sentiment was also promoted by the philanthropic works of civic-minded Hokkien *towkays* who catered to all dialect groups, regardless of their clan affiliation.[19]

# References/Notes

1. Kwa, C.G & Kua, B.L. (2019). *A General History of the Chinese in Singapore*. Singapore: World Scientific Publishing. p. 117.
2. Kwa & Kua. *Ibid*. p. 117.
3. Kwa & Kua. *Ibid*. p. 86.
4. *Annals of the Propagation of the Faith*, Vol. XLII, 10 September 1833.
5. Interview with Mr Philip Wee Peng Leng (1904–1991). Interviewed by Marjorie and Phyllis Wee on 18 August 1981. Personal collection.
6. Kwa & Kua. (2019). *A General History of the Chinese in Singapore*. pp. 37–46.
7. Trocki, C.A. (1990). *Opium and Empire: Chinese Society in Colonial Singapore, 1800–1910*. New York: Cornell University Press. p. 109.
8. *Directory of Straits Settlements*. (1873). Singapore: National Library Board.
9. Interview with Mr Philip Wee Peng Leng (1904–1991). Interviewed by Marjorie and Phyllis Wee on 18 August 1981. Personal collection.
10. Good Shepherd Church. Baptism Register 1832–1867. The actual date of the entry is unclear, but it appears to have taken place in late December 1839.
11. Rerceretnam, M. (2020). Intermarriage, religious conversions, and new Peranakans within multi-ethnic communities in colonial Singapore: The development of early multi-ethnic Roman Catholic communities, c. 1830s to 1860. In *Chapters on Asia (2019)*. Singapore: National Library Board.
12. Liew, C. (2016). *Persecution of Chinese Christians in Early Colonial Singapore 1845–1869*. Historical Inquiry Report, Roman Catholic Archdiocese of Singapore, (unpublished). p. 70.
13. Ong, O.S. (1902/1984). *100 Years History of the Chinese in Singapore*. pp. 40–41.
14. Trocki, C.A. *Opium and Empire. Chinese Society in Colonial Singapore, 1800–1910*. New York: Cornell University Press. p. 63; Kwa & Kua. (2019). *A General History of the Chinese in Singapore*. pp. 65–69.
15. Rerceretnam, M. (2020). Intermarriage, religious conversions, and new Peranakans within multi-ethnic communities in colonial Singapore: The development of early multi-ethnic Roman Catholic communities, c. 1830s to 1860. In *Chapters on Asia* (2019). Singapore: National Library Board.
16. Kwa & Kua (2019). *A General History of the Chinese in Singapore*. p. 60.
17. Liew. C. (2016). *Persecution of Chinese Christians in Early Colonial Singapore 1845–1869*. p. 63.
18. St Joseph's Church, Bukit Panjang. Liber Defunctorum (Deaths) 1846–1866. National Archives of Singapore. The records appear incomplete and sporadic. If up to 500 people died in the 1851 riots, these high numbers are not reflected in the church registers.
19. Kwa & Kua. (2019). *A General History of the Chinese in Singapore*. pp. 126–127.

Chapter 4

# Growth of Roman Catholic Businesses and Patronage

Chinese enterprise and business historically have played a key role in Singapore. There are several reasons for this. The colonial British needed a middleman for their economic regime to work to their advantage. They allowed and provided opportunities for Chinese businesses to intercede and act as middlemen. A role not offered to other racial groups. In other words, the British colonials facilitated the rise of various ethnic Chinese business empires to prominence. Chinese businesses needed British capital and British capital needed Chinese labour.[1] Like other Chinese businesses, Roman Catholic Chinese businesses found themselves provided with profitable opportunities and naturally many eagerly seized such opportunities.

By the end of the 1800s and the beginning of the 1900s, a relatively widespread and affluent Catholic business network was establishing itself. This new phenomenon encompassed small businesses and shops at the old Ellenborough Market, right up to large-scale and in many cases regional mercantile and banking businesses. These business networks were strongly tied to the Catholic church, and in a few cases were even a direct offshoot of the church. Heavy reliance on parishioner benefactors began in the 1840s, but especially so after 1873. The church was much envied for this widely recognised patronage. In 1907, Anglican pastor Reverend J. A. Bethune Cook claimed the Catholic church controlled 'a considerable number of the ordinary business houses in the name of Chinese traders and others', and as business corporations, 'their influence and wealth have increased.'[2] Other established churches such as the Anglican, Methodist and Presbyterian churches did not possess similar financially lucrative networks. However, Singapore's Catholic church did not achieve this fortunate position entirely by design.

## The Church needs cash

When the French Mission was first established in Singapore in 1832, its early lay congregation was largely made up of Roman Catholic Melaka Portuguese, recent arrivals from Melaka. They probably arrived soon after the establishment of the colonial outpost beginning from June 1819. Most were poor fisherfolk and fishmongers. The growing number of China-born Teochew converts were mainly poor labourers, farmhands, sole traders or small-scale farmers. They were followed by a smaller number of well-to-do Eurasians, some working as clerks in European firms, while others ran modest businesses. Most prominent in this group in the 1830s was I. J. Woodford, a pharmacist and church catechist, a well-known donor to the Catholic church. Other donors were a handful of parishioners of Irish descent: John Connolly, a shipping agent; Daniel Cunningham, a policeman; Joseph Melany, a merchant; Daniel McSwiney, a contractor and architect; George Godfrey, a tavern-owner, and A.F. Francis. When the decision was made to establish a small chapel on Bras Basah Road in 1832, donations were also sought from non-Catholics such as S.G. Bonham, later Resident of Singapore; A.L. Johnston; D.S. Napier and John Purvis, who were government officials and merchants and made one-off donations. Even the Portuguese Mission's Padre Francisco de Silva e Maia, who had staunchly opposed the establishment of the French Mission in Singapore, donated $20. Teochew parishioners and other 'subscribers' gave as much as $145.[3] At times, the priests donated their own money to keep initiatives going. In August 1852, Father Jean-Marie Beurel used $4,000 of his own money to buy the house at the corner of Victoria Street and Bras Basah Road to push ahead with the establishment of the Convent of the Holy Infant Jesus.[4]

The need to cover ongoing financial expenses relating to the growing church was great. Evangelistically speaking, Singapore offered a virtual *carte blanche* opportunity for the Catholic church. Most of its Protestant counterparts were concentrating on China.[5] As a result, the new Catholic church grew quickly in Singapore. It was in late December 1839, that thirty-one year-old Tan Nong Keah, already a wealthy merchant, was converted to the Catholic faith. His wealth and entrepreneurial skills arguably brought a new dynamic to the young and growing Roman Catholic parish. Tan was clearly the richest person affiliated to the church, followed only by a few middle-class Eurasians and Europeans, while the rest of the parishioners were generally poor. However, research for this book has uncovered a sizeable group of Teochew parishioners with small landholdings, farms, and small businesses, from around 1850:[6]

## Farmers

Tan Noh Tee[7] – Chan Chu Kang (today's Nee Soon village)
Kah Soon – Chan Chu Kang
Ong Oh – Mata Ikan (Changi/Somapah Village)
Ah Bee – Simpang (north of Yishun)
Nioh Ah Lim – Nam Toh Kang (Sembawang)
Tan Ah Toh – Nam Toh Kang
Ta Ah Tin – Geylang
Koh Sah Kee – Geylang
Sih Koh Tauw – Bookoh Kang/Bukho Kang (Mandai)
Tan Ah Yoh – Bukit Timah
Seng Choo – Lau Choo Kang (Sungei Kadut, near Mandai)
Tjoo Ah Len – Kranji
Tan Ah Tee – area unknown
Paul Ah Koon – Bookoh Kang/Bukho Kang (Mandai)
Philip Teo Ho Kah – area unknown
Tan Chye Kweh – boatman, Ellenborough New Market, Clarke Quay
Lauw Ah Tang – shop owner, Ellenborough New Market, Clarke Quay.

Most of the Teochews' farming interest centred around gambier and pepper cultivation at the time. This seems also to have applied to the Catholic Teochews. Their farms were spread across the rural parts of Singapore, from west to east, but a majority appear to have been concentrated in the north-western section of the island, in the Nee Soon/ Yishun, Sembawang, Mandai and Kranji districts.

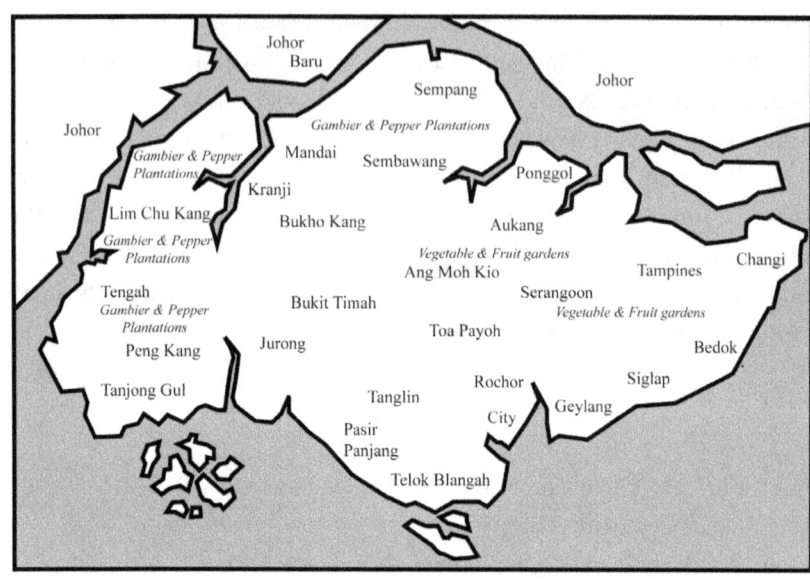

*Singapore in 1885*

## The 1892 Saints Peter & Paul's Church benefactors' marble tablet

In 2015, during renovations at the Saints Peter & Paul's Church in Queen Street, an old wall-mounted marble tablet, hidden by previous renovations, was rediscovered. It was originally unveiled in 1892 and appears to provide a list of major parish benefactors from the Teochew congregation since the church's inception in the 1830s, although this does not appear to be its sole purpose. According to church archival records, between 1891 and 1892, the church was enlarged when the sacristy and transept were built. The parish priest at the time, Father Alphonse Vignol, also erected three marble altars. This author believes some of the listed names relate directly to these new building works in 1892. The priest was also keen to recognise past benefactors and so included other longer-term benefactors on this list.

The content of the three tablets appears to be classifiable as two distinct sections. The first section (occupying the centre of the tablet) contains seven columns of names, the most prominent names being listed at the top. The second section is located on the left and right of the tablet,

*Benefactors' tablet, Saints Peter & Paul's Church, 1892*

Source: Chancery of the Roman Catholic Archdiocese of Singapore

and appears to identify the purpose of this tablet. The left-hand column; 天主降生一千八百九十二年本堂神父衛重修立 translates as 'Solemnly erected by the priests of the parish in the 1892nd year of the Lord, in commemoration of the restoration of the church'. The right-hand column 將壬辰年增修聖堂信友喜捐題芳名開列於左 translates as 'Here in the year of Ren Chen (Water Dragon), are listed on the left the illustrious names of the faithful, who joyfully donated to the additions to the church.'

The middle section of the tablets holds seven columns of names:

*1st column (read left to right) lists the following —*
Tan Nong Keah (陳奴仔)
Chan Teck Hee (曾德意)
Cheong Quee Theam (鐘貴添)
Ang Kiam Moh (洪謙茂) – business
Yong Lee Seng (永利成) – business.

*2nd column (read left to right) —*
Lee Ah Peng (李亞丙)
Yong Hoa Seng (永和成) – business
Yong Chia Hong (永洽豐) – business
Seng Yong Cheng (成永清) –business
Kwang Seng Cheong (廣成昌) – business
Lim Yong Seng (林永盛).

*3rd column (read left to right) —*
Low Kiok Chiang (盧克昌)
Tan Jee Tou (陳二吐)
Goh Ngee Kee (吳義記)
Goh Liang Hup (吳兩合)
Lee Soon Kheng (李順慶)
Tay Hup Huat (鄭合發)
Cheng Hock Hup (鐘富合).

*4th column (read left to right) —*
All the faithful at the New (Ellenborough) Market (新吧虱 眾信友)
Ng Yong Seng (黃榮盛)
Teo Yeng Seng (張延生)
Tan Kwang Joo (陳廣裕)
Kiam Hoa Heng (謙和成) – business
Tan Jin Hup (陳仁合).

*5th column (read left to right) —*
Chop Guan Chuan (源泉號) – business
Buan Hoa Seng (萬和盛) – business
Lee Kiah Soon (李加順)
Ong Ker Keng (王居乾)
Loh Boon Kao (盧文高)
Ng Moh Huat (黃茂發)
Chop Teck Seng (德盛號) business.

*6th column (read left to right) —*
Teo Cheng Chew (張鎮卅)
Lee Yong Soon (李永順)
Chia Meng Chiong (謝明昌)
Lim Teck Loong (林德閏)
Boon Weng Ker (文苑衢)
Chai Kee Leng (蔡麒麟)
Ng Choon Seng (黃崇成).

*7th column (read left to right) —*
Ong Meng Seng (王銘成)
Chop Swee Seng (瑞盛號)
Seet Tua Tee (薛大弟)
Chop Chee Seng (致成號) – business
Chao Kee Meng (曹啟明).

*Source: Chinese to English script translation by Alex Yam and John Tan, 28 August & 16 September 2019.*

## The Ellenborough 'New Market', Clarke Quay

Apart from affluent benefactors, an unusual mention of a non-descript group catches the eye in the fourth column on these tablets. On the 1892 benefactors' list, special reference is made to 'All the faithful at the New Market' (新吧虱　眾信友). The 'New Market' (新吧虱) or *Pasar Bahru* in Malay, refers to the former Ellenborough Market, which was located on today's New Market Road, near Clarke Quay MRT station. This 'wet' market (typically, tropical Asian fresh markets have wet floors, from keeping produce iced, cool and clean) was built in 1845 (and extended in 1899 with another structure on its side), named after Lord Ellenborough, the then Governor-General of India (1841–1844). It soon became a well-known Teochew enclave specialising in fresh fish, dried seafood products and Teochew cuisine. The whole Boat Quay area was known as a Teochew enclave from the first half of the nineteenth century, and as a result, the market was also nicknamed 'Teochew Market'. It was a success from its inception[8] and by the 1960s, there were approximately 1,000 hawkers and stallholders housed at the venue, until it was destroyed by a fire in January 1968.[9]

Ellenborough Market, or 'New Market' (1845–1968)

Source: National Archives Singapore

No information exists that can help identify how many Teochew Roman Catholics were at this market, although it is clear that a sizeable Teochew Catholic component existed. To illustrate this point, in September 1862, anti-Roman Catholic placards were specially posted at this market by Teochew secret societies, decrying the activities of the church and, according to the *Straits Times* (4 October 1862), also putting a $1,000 reward on the head of French priest, Father Augustine Périé.[10]

Since there were probably a large number of Catholic stallholders at the Ellenborough Market, these sole-traders and small businessmen probably collectively contributed considerable amounts of money (in relation to their assets) to the church. The author currently is only able to identify two of them, active around 1850: Lauw Ah Tang who ran a stall and Tan Chye Kweh, a boatman operating just outside the market. Just as the Ellenborough Market's Teochew stallholders would have supported their church, in later years, similar workplace collective fundraising initiatives were seen, such as the drive to build St Teresa's Church in Kampong Bahru, where a substantial sum was donated by the 'Rickshaw-Pullers of Muar Road' in 1925.[11]

## The philanthropic first wave, 1840–1880: Pedro Tan Nong Keah

Although the marble tablets are dated 1892, they appear not to be specific to that year. The names listed acknowledge and identify past benefactors going back to the 1840s. Pedro Tan Nong Keah's name takes pride of place at the top of the list, even though he had died six years previously, in 1886. Current research shows Pedro Tan was the primary benefactor in the first wave of Catholic church philanthropists, probably holding this position until the 1880s. As a long-term parishioner, Tan was relied on as a funding source on numerous occasions.

Contributions to the church were solicited from all levels of Singapore society, rich and poor, Catholic and

*Father Jean-Marie Beurel (1813-1872)*
Source: *Chancery of the Roman Catholic Archdiocese of Singapore*

non-Catholic, with even the priests themselves, such as Father Jean-Marie Beurel, giving from their own pockets to ensure church-related projects went ahead. At the cash-starved Portuguese Mission, construction of their own church in 1853 was largely made possible thanks to the late Padre Maia's bequest of his assets to the church.

Father John Tschu, who was the first to befriend Tan when he converted to Catholicism 1839, was quick to describe him as a 'wealthy' merchant. As already mentioned, with his plantation rights in Singapore and at several locations in Johore, his Boat Quay shop, his opium and remittance business, Tan was indeed a wealthy man. It was no wonder the church welcomed him with open arms. The arrival of Tan in the church changed the face of its fundraising, previously reliant on the humble offerings from its own congregation, small grants from the colonial government and even general contributions from benefactors not connected with the church.

As described earlier, in 1863, Father Augustine Périé (1832–1892) used Tan's financial backing to lease an area in Pontian Kechil, Johore, but had to back out of the project because he had underestimated his operational costs. Tan also quit the investment, much to Périé's disenchantment.[12]

*Father Augustine Périé (1832–1892)*
Source: Chancery of the Roman Catholic Archdiocese of Singapore

## The philanthropic second wave, 1880s–1930: Small and large businesses emerge

It was only from the 1880s, especially in the 1890s, that a second wave of Catholic philanthropists emerged. Its main protagonist was a Bangkok-based mercantile enterprise called Kiam Hoa Heng (謙和成) founded around 1878. The story of how this venture was originally established starts with a new arrival in about 1857, Saints Peter & Paul's church parishioner, Jacobe Low Kiok Chiang (盧克昌) (1843–1911). Low was born in 1843 in the village of Swalek/Xialiecun (仙乐) in Shantou city (Swatow) on the southern coast of China. He left China with his older brother Benedict Low Kiok Liang around 1857. Jacobe got a job with MEP in the late 1850s or early 1860s at the Mission's former headquarters located at the corner of River Valley and Oxley Roads. He initially worked as a cook, but by the 1860s was working as a banking assistant for the MEP administration. He converted to Catholicism at the age of twenty. Father Augustine Périé recognised Low's business acumen and saw an opportunity, so he arranged for MEP to provide a loan or grant of $1,000 to the younger Low to start up a mercantile business in Bangkok (Siam/Thailand), which became the Kiam Hoa Heng company.

*Advertisement, Kiam Hoa Heng & Co., 1903*

Source: Business Directory of the Straits Settlements and Singapore, 1903

Soon after, Jacobe Low got a fellow Saints Peter & Paul's church parishioner and childhood friend hailing from a neighbouring village in Low's hometown area of Shantou, Joseph Chan Teck Hee (曾德意) (1844–1930), to join him in this venture. Both Low and Chan relocated with their young families to Bangkok and working with the MEP office there, soon got themselves established. Kiam Hoa Heng (謙和成) enterprise became a successful entity and quickly expanded to encompass over half a dozen companies, located in Bangkok, Singapore, and even in Shantou. Apart from the primary Kiam Hoa Heng business, which was on the grounds of the Holy Rosary Church in the Samphanthawong District of Bangkok, on the eastern bank of the Chao Phraya River, there were Buan Hoa Seng (萬和盛), Gin Hong Hoa Kee and Kiam Hoa Siang, all also in Bangkok, as well as Yong Hoa Seng (永和成) (Singapore) and Kiam Hoa Heng Hua Kee (Shantou). Kiam Hoa Heng in Bangkok became so prominent that the Siamese royal court accorded it the prestigious royal warranty to display the royal coat of arms, from the 1890s.

One of several branches of the Kiam Hoa Heng enterprise in Bangkok, c. 1910

Source: Low family descendants

Around the 1880s and the 1890s, Jacobe Low and Joseph Chan began redirecting large sums of money from their firms into the Catholic church. The MEP itself, based in the Bangrak district of Bangkok, was a minor shareholder in the Kiam Hoa Heng company. As to exactly how much Low and Chan financially contributed, and for what purposes, this will probably never be fully known. Apparently, no accurate accounts or records have survived. However, family sources claim both Low and Chan were devoted, humble and pious Catholics who probably saw their financial success as the direct result of God's grace. Giving back to the church with generosity was therefore a natural response for them.

*The Holy Rosary Church, Bangkok*
Source: Low family descendants

According to Low family sources, most of these contributions were destined for the building and renovation of church and associated mission schools in Singapore. However, the Lows' efforts were not concentrated in Singapore alone, but spread also to Siam, and Shantou in China. One of their first large-scale philanthropic ventures was the construction of the Holy Rosary Church in Bangkok. Construction began in 1891 and continued till 1897.

Bangkok church records accurately show funding for the build came primarily from Kiam Hoa Heng-associated companies and the families connected with the companies. Low family sources confirm this, saying that family members were obliged to take huge cuts to their personal allowances during the six-year build. According to family members,

*Father Desalles (left) with Jacobe Low Kiok Chiang (middle) and children at the newly completed Holy Rosary Church in Bangkok, around 1897*

Source: Low family descendants

Jacobe Low was reluctant to give money to his family, preferring to donate it to the church:

> ... my grandfather, Low Kiok Chiang, he gave half of his property to the church ... he said "Children don't need so much money. You give them too much money, who knows, they might turn bad" (laughter).
>
> Source: Interview with Marie Cheng Mui Kiang (née Goh), 1921–2003, granddaughter of Jacobe Low Kiok Chiang, 22 January 1997.

In the same vein, Joseph Chan was described by clergy as:

*... an example of simplicity, humility, generosity and piety. If ever you met him, you would never have thought he was a rich man. Shod in slippers, he used to sweep the church, the presbytery, and the drains of the houses of the poor, which stood on the site of the present Catholic High School of the Church Ss. Peter and Paul.*

Source: St Teresa's Souvenir, *Jubilee Issue*, October 1954, p. 25.

In another project, Low and Chan purchased land in the Lam Sai Sub district near Bangkok in January 1897 and donated it to the church. This was done to allow local farmer parishioners to work on rice cultivation plots near their parish church. In 1897, back in Singapore, Chan bought land adjoining the Saints Peter & Paul's church and built eleven houses for church catechists, local widows and the aged. This row of houses became known as the St Joseph's houses. Both Low and Chan also commissioned Belgium-made stained-glass windows for the Church of Saints Peter & Paul around this same time.

*The stained-glass windows, Saints Peter & Paul's Church, Singapore*
Source: Chancery of the Roman Catholic Archdiocese of Singapore

In 1901, Low and his family paid for the construction of another Holy Rosary church, this time in their Teochew family village of Swalek in China. In 1909, Chan and Low helped fund the reconstruction and renovation of Bangkok's Assumption Cathedral. The work took nine years to complete. In 1910, the two men were pivotal in the purchase of land and the construction of the Church of the Sacred Heart on Tank Road in Singapore. This church was allocated to the 'Khek' - (Hakka) and Cantonese-speaking congregations. In 1925, the Kiam Hoa Heng company bought land and constructed buildings for Bangkok's Carmelite Convent. In 1929, contributions were made to finance the construction of the Church of St Teresa in Singapore.[13]

Low family descendants at the Holy Rosary Church, Swalek, Shantou, China
2 December 2019

Source: Mr Low Yeow Teng

Apart from these major projects, the Lows and Chans regularly donated smaller amounts to various Catholic projects such as schools in both Singapore and Siam. The link between the Catholic church and these businesses was a well-known fact among rival religious communities by the early 1900s.[14]

*Jacobe Low Kiok Chiang (1843-1911)*  
Source: Low family descendants

*Joseph Chan Teck Hee (1844-1930)*  
Source: Marie Chan

From around 1900, a third philanthropist joined the ranks alongside Low and Chan. Cheng Quee Thiam (鐘貴添) (1839–1914) was the proprietor of a pawnbroking firm called Chop Eng Whatt, located at 126 South Bridge Road. His business was not as large or prominent as Low or Chan's enterprises. However, Cheng appeared to be as generous as his two compatriots and matched their contributions. He was one of three major contributors to the Saints Peter & Paul's church and Sacred Heart Church in Singapore, up to 1910.

Cheng and Chan both enjoyed strong links with the wider non-Christian Teochew business community. In 1907, they were founding members of the Sze Hai Tong Banking and Insurance Company Limited or Four Seas Bank (四海通). Cheng served on the Board of Directors until his death in 1914 and Chan until 1930. After their deaths, their sons Cheng Guan Swee and Chan Chin Kwang, took up positions as bank directors from the 1920s. The Sze Hai Tong Bank was one of the earliest banks in Singapore, founded by prominent members of the Teochew Taoist clan organisation. Several other Roman Catholics served on the bank's Board of Directors over the years, including Chong Thutt Pitt, Cheng Khye Yong (1866–1932) and Andrew Goh Yong Joo (1880–1939).

Sze Hai Tong Bank, Board of Directors and staff, 1927

Source: National Archives Singapore

Andrew Goh Yong Joo was a shareholder in Kiam Hoa Heng and the General Manager of Kiam Hoa Heng sister company Buan Hoa Seng (萬和盛) in Bangkok, from around 1900 to 1931. He was also a son-in-law of Jacobe Low Kiok Chiang. In Singapore in the 1930s, Goh was personally approached by Teochew clan leader and Sze Hai Tong Bank founder Lee Wee Nam (1881–1964), a non-Christian, to take a position on the Board of Directors.[15] The Sze Hai Tong Bank was acquired by the Oversea-Chinese Banking Corporation (OCBC) in 1972 and was finally merged with the OCBC in July 1998.[16]

The Singapore church's philanthropic reach was not confined to the island, Bangkok or southern China alone. China-born Goh Ah Ngee arrived in Singapore around 1850 and lived in Queen Street. He had worked as a pioneer in the Selangor tin industry, peninsular Malaya from as early as the 1870s. He later dabbled in rubber plantations. It is claimed he was one of the first Chinese to settle in Kuala Lumpur after the British Residency moved there from Klang in 1880.[17] He was also a major benefactor of the original Church of St John the Evangelist when it was first established in 1883, and of the CHIJ Convent Bukit Nanas in Kuala Lumpur, which first opened its doors in 1899.[18] Goh may have died in the late 1920s or early 1930s. Although originally from Singapore, his philanthropy apparently manifested itself only in Selangor, Kuala Lumpur and Negeri Sembilan, Malaya.[19]

During the first wave of Catholic philanthropy (1840–1880), Catholic-run businesses essentially were small sole trader set-ups. Many were run by a family member in places like the Ellenborough Market. By the 1900s, proper shops and small businesses were becoming common. Companies like Yong Lee Seng and Seng Yong Cheng sold liquor and other beverages. Kwang Seng Cheong, Ang Kiam Moh, Chop Thiam Soon Hong, Chop Kwang Joo, Chop Guan Chuan, Chop Teck Seng, Chop Swee Seng and Chop Chee Seng were mercantile enterprises, wholesalers, and retailers. By this point, we can also observe a diversification outside the Teochew community, with several firms run by Cantonese and Hokkiens.

Goh Ah Ngee, pioneer tin miner and Kuala Lumpur church philanthropist
Source: Cheng family descendants

## The philanthropic third wave, 1930–1945: Grassroots organising, more businesses arise

There is considerable overlap between the second and third philanthropic waves in the Catholic community of Singapore. Joseph Chan Teck Hee (1844–1930), whose role as a church philanthropist spanned six decades, died in 1930. It was Chan and Low who had taken over the philanthropic baton from Pedro Tan in the 1880s. However, the dynamics of the third wave were not too different from that of the second. There was still a large disparity in wealth between the different philanthropists, but there was a considerable increase in the number of successful small to medium-sized enterprises. By the 1930s, the advent of the Great Depression and new developments in the mercantile business market together saw the Kiam Hoa Heng company on the wane. And with the passing of Low in 1911 and eventually Chan in 1930, the Kiam Hoa Heng enterprises lost much of their philanthropic drive and zeal.

This period also witnessed the rise of a new kind of church dynamic: most significantly, the rise of the local grassroots church activist organisation, overseen by local-born clergy. Parishioners like Lee Kheng Guan, the owner of Chop Lee Kheng Hong, based at 258 River Valley Road, were key in this development. Lee Kheng Guan's main contribution was the pivotal work he and his family did with projects and campaigns associated with Father Stephen Lee. As a continuation from the second wave's Chan Teck Hee and Cheng Quee Tiam's involvement with the wider Teochew community, the Lees were active participants in non-Christian, mainstream organisations such as the Huilai Countrymen Association, the Teochew Poit Ip Huay Kuan (潮州八邑會館), the Teoyeonh Huay Kuan, and significantly, in the Huilai Refugee Representative Committee. They played a pivotal organisational role in the 1928 repatriation of a few hundred Catholic refugees escaping their war-torn town of Peknay (百冷乡) in China. Many were resettled in the Mandai region of Singapore with the help of the church and benefactors.[20]

*Paul Lee Kheng Guan and Lee Kheng Seng c. 1920s*

Source: Cyprian Lim

In the second wave (1880s–1930) while much of the cash came from a handful of Teochew firms, the bulk of the donated funds was used under the direction of French MEP clergy. By the 1920s, this changed. This new dynamic was clearly played out in the drive to build the Church of St Teresa from 1925. Young enterprising local-born priests like Father Stephen Lee Boon Teck (1895–1955) came to the fore. Probably through Joseph Chan Teck Hee and Cheng Quee Thiam, Father Lee formed strong links with non-Catholic business elites at the time. Father Lee knew Sze Hai Tong Bank founder, Lee Wee Nam, and through him arranged for many of his parishioners to invest or buy shares in the bank. Father Lee was also acquainted with other prominent local sharebrokers like J. M. Sassoon (who was Jewish), who upon his request, helped invest on behalf of Father Lee's parishioners too.[21]

Father Stephen Lee Boon Teck
(1895–1955)

Source: Chancery of the Roman Catholic Archdiocese of Singapore

Lee Wee Nam in 1924 (1881–1964), founder of the Sze Hai Tong Banking and Insurance Company

Source: National Archives Singapore

Other Catholic businesses were small but well known. Saints Peter & Paul's church parishioners like Glasgow-trained, medical practitioner, Dr Peter Chia Teck Yam (1900–1989), owned and ran the Hinnam & Little Pharmacy at North Bridge Road from the late 1920s. Augustine Chia Meng Chiang owned and ran Chop Chia Meng, an undertaker's business which was taken over by his brother, on the event of Augustine's premature death in the 1910s.[22] There was another Catholic undertaker's business, a much bigger concern called Singapore Casket, still operating today.[23] That firm, run by a Eurasian Catholic family, the Hochstadts, was established in 1920. China-born merchant John Lee Khiah Soon (1855–1927), also known as a 'millionaire of Orchard Road', owned the successful Chop Tien Seng Chan Oil Trading Company and Tiang Seng Chan (天成) located on Orchard and Beach Roads in the 1890s. Lee arrived in Singapore in 1887 and began working for a Teochew Roman Catholic family from 1887, run by China-born Cheng Ah Foo and his Borneo (West Kalimantan)-born Peranakan wife Anna Low Soon Neo (1831–1926). By the 1900s, the Cheng family business, Chop Kwang Hwa Hong, was being run by their son John Baptist Cheng Kye Yong (1866–1932) at 81 Rochore Road, a moneylending, hardware and paint retail business. John Lee Khiah Soon married into the Cheng family.

Other examples were Lee Soon Kheng (1857–c.1930), a wealthy Ponggol resident and merchant; Lim Koon Heng, who owned a large provision shop at 55 Orchard Road; Andrew Goh Yong Joo (1880–1939) and his two sons, Joseph (1905–1944) and Philip (1908–1944), who ran YJ Goh & Sons (also known as Andrew Goh & Sons) which he established in 1934. Singapore-born Goh moved permanently back to Singapore from Bangkok in 1932 and had previously run Buan Hoa Seng in Bangkok from around 1900. His father John Goh Ah Seng (1851–1916) ran the same business after it was established by second-wave Catholic philanthropists Jacobe Low Kiok Chiang and Joseph Chan Teck Hee in 1883. In Singapore, Andrew Goh's import-export business dealt in a variety of goods and building materials but were primarily ship chandlers. They also specialised in the importation of tubular steel Art Deco-style furniture from Czechoslovakia.

The Heng family were western-educated Teochew medical practitioners, who established a clinic on Armenia Street around the early 1900s. Over the decades they expanded their clinics, now renamed 'Wilma Clinic' around Singapore, their biggest venture was their original clinic, located on Armenia Street. Some members of the Heng family married into the abovementioned Goh family, who ran Bangkok's Buan Hoa Seng business entreprise from the 1880s onwards.

Growth of Roman Catholic Businesses and Patronage  85

*Andrew Goh Yong Joo (1880–1939) and wife, Veronica Low Kim Luan (1887–1976)*
Source: Goh & Low family descendants

---

Telephone No. 7843.

**THE VICTORIA CONFECTIONERY & STORE**
Wedding Cakes a Speciality
Assorted Cakes Maker, Tea Party Supplier,
Hot and Cold Drinks, etc.

71, Victoria Street,
SINGAPORE.

*Proprietor*
JOSEPH CHONG SIN TONG

---

*Advertisement for the Victoria Confectionery & Store*
Source: Malayan Catholic Leader, 30 March 1935, Vol. 01, No. 13, p. 17

Sacred Heart church parishioner Peter Chong, had his Peter Chong Stationery shop on Bras Basah Road and was the official book retailer for all Roman Catholic mission schools in Singapore. Joseph Chong Sin Tong (decd 1942) owned and ran the Victoria Confectionery and Store at 71 Victoria Street from around 1916. The store also supplied cakes and refreshments to important church-related events.[24]

Joseph Chong was popularly known as 'Ah Teng' and lived a street down from his business at 2 Queen Street. He was a keen supporter of the Cantonese Hoi Thin Association. His eldest son Paul married Rosa da Luz, daughter of the long-time parish registrar at St Joseph's Church (Portuguese Mission) in 1934. Apart from the bakery, Chong also had considerable landholdings in Bukit Timah and Balmoral, and owned 61 Waterloo Street, which is today part of the Roman Catholic Chancery. Chong donated $3,300 towards the St Teresa's Church building fund in 1927.[25]

*The Church of St Teresa, Kampong Bahru*

*Source: Chancery of the Roman Catholic Archdiocese of Singapore*

In the late 1920s and early 1930s, key philanthropists played a prominent role in the fundraising and construction of the Church of St Teresa located at Kampong Bahru. At the time, the proposed church was reported to be the largest Roman Catholic church building in the Archdiocese of Singapore. It was as large and ambitious as it was expensive.

'Orchard Road millionaire' John Lee Kiah Soon (1854–1927) ran rubber plantations, moneylending services, and was an agent for Socony-Vacuum Oil Company (later Mobil Oil). His shop, Chop Tiang Seng Chan (天成). was a supplier to the General Hospital and the British army. He also owned 'The French Bakery' located on Kramat Road. Lee probably started donating toward Roman Catholic causes from the early 1890s. In the 1920s, he contributed $10,000 towards the St Teresa's Church building fund.[26]

Peter Lim Ah Pin (1890—1943) was a well-known vermicelli manufacturer and was popularly known as 'the Bee Hoon King' in the early twentieth century. Before he found his fortune as an entrepreneur, he worked as a bus conductor and a fruit seller. There are streets named after him and his wife, Florence, in Upper Serangoon Road, Hougang area. Lim arrived in Singapore from southern China's Fujian province as a teenager and, at the age of nineteen, married a seventeen-year-old Peranakan girl Florence Yeo, whom he met at the CHIJ Convent orphanage. Peter and Florence contributed generously to the construction of St Teresa's Sino-English School and the Cannossian Convent in Aljunied Road.[27]

*Peter Lim Ah Pin (1890-1943) and Florence Yeo (1887-1962)*

Source: Des Sim

Money from older sources linked with first- (1840–1880s) and second-wave (1880s–1930) philanthropists was still dominant. Kiam Hoa Heng's Joseph Chan Teck Hee (1844–1930) gave $50,000. Chan's wife Mary Koh gave an additional $6,100.[28]

Chan's collaborator and friend, Jacobe Low Kiok Chiang, died in 1911, but his legacy was carried on by his eldest son and then a British resident, Philip Julian Low Gek Seng (1869–1945) who gave $20,000.

Another key philanthropist was a relative newcomer to the scene. David Wee Cheng Soon (1875–1944) had been a key donor to the Catholic church and mission

*Maria Koh*

Source: Marie Chan

*A formal blessing from Pope Pius X (St Pius X) to Philip Julian Low Gek Seng when Low had a private audience during a visit to the Vatican in 1912. Low had at least two more private meetings with Popes Benedict XV and possibly Pius XI in the following years*

Source: Dorothy Salvi (née Low)

schools from at least 1911. He was a building contractor specialising in the construction of roads, military installations and government buildings. His business only became successful from late 1904, four years after its establishment, so Wee was a relatively late entry into the philanthropy scene.[29]

Wee had an interesting background. He was the grandson of Pedro Tan Nong Keah (1808–1886), the original parishioner philanthropist of 1839. He was a descendant from Pedro Tan's first marriage to local woman Joanna An Gau in 1841. After Joanna's premature death in 1847, Tan remarried to Anna Lim Ah

*David Wee Cheng Soon (1875-1944)*

Source: Wee family descendants

Keow several years later and proceeded to start a new family.[30] Little is known of Tan's relationship with his children from earlier relationships, although it is clear that they did not enjoy close ties, certainly not in business. By the time David Wee Cheng Soon was born in 1875, the Wees seemed to have no contact with Pedro Tan.

David Wee Cheng Soon was the son of Victoria Tan Choo Lan (1843–1910), daughter of Pedro Tan. According to church records and newspaper reports, Victoria's half-brother and David's uncle, John Tan Hay Seng (c.1847–1902) was also a Catholic philanthropist, although no direct accounts of his contributions to church causes survive. John Tan was the original concessionaire of the Pahang Mining Corporation, also a timber merchant, and had a fleet of ships and various other sea-craft. In his younger days, he was one of a handful of students mentored by Father Jean-Marie Beurel when the priest established St Joseph's Institution in 1852. Unfortunately, John's fortunes turned sour in the 1890s and he died destitute in 1902. His sister Victoria married China-born rice merchant Wee (Ng) Ah Soi in the 1860s and the couple had nine children together. They had first met at their local catechism class. She lived at the family home at 3 River Valley Road until her death in 1910.[31] Although David

Wee Cheng Soon received little benefit from the fortunes of his wealthy grandfather, they appeared to share a commitment to the Catholic church. In fact, David Wee Cheng Soon was probably more committed to the church than his grandfather Pedro Tan was. According to an article written in 1954, a decade after Wee's death:

> ... it appears that in sponsoring the cause of charity, giving till it hurts was his guiding principle ...
>
> "From God, it comes ... and to God it should go". He saw God in the poor, the homeless and the starving.
>
> Source: St Teresa's Souvenir, *Jubilee Issue*, October 1954, p. 24

Wee Cheng Soon business advertisement
Source: St Joseph's Institution Annual 1922. SJI archives

In 1926, during the early stages of planning for the new Church of St Teresa, costs amounting to over $211,000 stood in the way of Bishop Rt. Rev. E. Barrillon signing the building contract. The Bishop was afraid the church fundraisers would fall short of their needed target. Joseph Chan Teck Hee and David Wee Cheng Soon came to the rescue when they advanced the needed cash. Between Chan and Wee, they were able to guarantee a sum of $202,000, just a few thousands short of the target amount. David Wee Cheng Soon's own contribution towards the fund was $30,000.[32] Bishop Barrillon was happy with this and authorised the signing of the contract.

With the calamity of the Japanese invasion of Singapore in February 1942, many local businesses, unprepared for the chaos of war, fell apart. During the Occupation, fortunes were confiscated by the Japanese military, and business activity collapsed. During the war years (1942–1945), the now ageing Wee Cheng Soon remained in Singapore, and with his son, Philip Wee Peng Leng (1904–1991) continued to provide food to convents and their orphanages, while paying and housing their employees (probably numbering between 100 to 200) despite their business not operating.[33] Wee Cheng Soon passed away on the 21st of April 1944 at the age of 69. By the 24th of May 1944, the company and family coffers were depleted, and son Philip Wee Peng Leng, was forced to sell off much of the family jewellery to continue supporting the estate, employees, renters and church networks.

*Philip Wee Peng Leng (1904-1991)*
Source: Wee family descendants

The years following the return of the British colonials were similarly bleak. The British government itself was bankrupt and little was left for colonies like Singapore. Government infrastructure and contracts dried up. Many large businesses were forced to liquidate. By 1950, the Wee business had collapsed.

By the end of the war, what little was left was divided by surviving family members. Many did not share the entrepreneurial zeal that drove their parents' generation. The Catholic business and philanthropic networks dwindled and the great fortunes of the past were never regenerated.

## Reference/Notes

1. Trocki, C.A. (1990). *Opium and Empire: Chinese Society in Colonial Singapore, 1800-1910*. New York: Cornell University Press. p. 5.
2. Cook, J.A. Bethune. (1907). *Sunny Singapore: An Account of the Place and its People with a Sketch of the Results of Missionary Work*. London: Elliot Stock. p. 134.
3. Buckley, C.B. *An Anecdotal History of Old Times in Singapore (1819-1867)*. (1902/1984). p. 245.
4. Convent of the Holy Infant Jesus. (1983/2003). *C.H.I.J. Victoria Street 1854-1983* (Singapore: CHIJ/NLB). p. 14.
5. Ackerman, S., & Lee, R. (1988). *Heaven in Transition*. Honolulu: University of Hawaii Press. pp. 29, 38; Loh, K.A. (1963). *Fifty years of the Anglican Church in Singapore Island 1909-1959*. Singapore: University of Singapore. p. 5..
6. Anonymous. 'Local'. In *The Singapore Free Press and Mercantile Advertiser*, 21 February 1851. p. 2. http://eresources.nlb.gov.sg/newspapers/Digitised/Article/singfreepressa18510221-1.2.7 accessed on 13 February 2019.
7. Trocki, CA. (1979/2007). *Prince of Pirates: The Temenggongs and the Development of Johor and Singapore 1784-1885*. Singapore: NUS Press. p. 221.Tan Noh Tee is listed as a Kangchu in Pontian Kechil, Johore, May 1866.
8. Anonymous. The Free Press. In *The Singapore Free Press and Mercantile Advertiser*, 31 May 1849, p. 2. http://eresources.nlb.gov.sg/newspapers/Digitised/Article/singfreepressa18490531-1.2.5 accessed on 16 September 2019.
9. Cornelius, V. (1999). Ellenborough Market. In *Singapore Infopedia*. https://eresources.nlb.gov.sg/infopedia/articles/SIP_480_2005-01-07.html accessed on 17 September 2019.
10. Anonymous. News of the Week. In *The Straits Times*, 4 October 1862, p. 1. http://eresources.nlb.gov.sg/newspapers/Digitised/Article/straitstimes18621004-1.2.6 accessed on 20 September 2019.
11. Anonymous. October 1954. *St Teresa's Souvenir, Jubilee Issue*. Singapore: Church of St Teresa.
12. Guerassimoff, E. (1997). The gangzhu of Johor: Memories of a French missionary in Malaysia 1859-1870. In *Études Chinoises*, Vol. XVI, No. 1, 1997. p. 127.
13. Interview with Ms Teresa Goh Mui Imm (1913-1995) and Mrs Marie Cheng Mui Kiang (née Goh) (1921-2003). Interviewed by Marc Rerceretnam, May 1988. Personal collection. Information provided by Songsak Tobsbowon of Bangkok, 23 January 2018.
14. Cook, J. A. Bethune. (1907). *Sunny Singapore*. p. 134.
15. Interview with Stephen Cheng Chin Mong (1919-1999) and Mrs Marie Cheng Mui Kiang (née Goh) (1921-2003). Interviewed by Marc Rerceretnam, 22 January 1997. Personal collection. Goh was approached by Sze Hai Tong Bank founder Lee Wee Nam, at his home in Katong.
16. Chia Y.J., Joshua. (2019). Sze Hai Tong Banking & Insurance Company Limited. *Singapore Infopedia*, 2019. Singapore: National Library Board. https://eresources.nlb.gov.sg/infopedia/articles/SIP_1162_2008-10-28.html accessed on 10 November 2019.

17 'Kuala Lumpur Correspondent'. The Moving Finger Writes – A Memorable Conversation – Towkay Goh Ah Gnee and a new Councillor – The Symbolic Dover Sole – In defence of the Malay. *A Journal in the Federal Capital*. In *The Straits Times*, 29 July 1933. p. 19. http://eresources.nlb.gov.sg/newspapers/Digitised/Article/straitstimes19330729-1.2.160 accessed 20 February 2020. This account of Goh Ah Ngee's life is given by his son-in-law, Lai Tet Loke, who was the Chinese member on the Federal Council in 1933.

18 Anonymous. History of the Church. In *Cathedral of St John the Evangelist*, Kuala Lumpur. http://www.stjohnkl.com.my/about-us/history-of-the-church accessed 20 February 2020; Anonymous. Convent Bukit Nanas'. https://en.wikipedia.org/wiki/Convent_Bukit_Nanas accessed 20 February 2020.

19 Anonymous. The First Church … Church of the Visitation, Seremban. In *Herald Malaysia Online*, 6 October 2014. http://www.heraldmalaysia.com/news/the-first-church-church-of-the-visitation-seremban/21080/5 accessed 21 February 2020.

20 Lim, C. (2019). *My Maternal Roots: A Story of Family, Faith and Freedom*. Singapore: World Scientific Press. pp. 129–135, 149–158.

21 Interview with Stephen Cheng Chin Mong (1919–1999) and Marie Cheng Mui Kiang (née Goh) (1921–2003). Interviewed by Marc Rerceretnam, 22 January 1997. Personal collection.

22 Interview with Stephen Cheng Chin Mong (1919–1999) and Mrs Marie Cheng Mui Kiang (née Goh) (1921–2003). Interviewed by Marc Rerceretnam, 22 January 1997. Personal collection.

23 Singapore Casket Company (Pte) Ltd. *About Us*. https://www.singaporecasket.com.sg/about-us/history-and-milestones/ accessed 1 February 2020.

24 Interview with Stephen Cheng Chin Mong (1919–1999) and Marie Cheng Mui Kiang (née Goh) (1921–2003). Interviewed by Marc Rerceretnam, 22 January 1997. Personal collection.

25 Interview with Stephen Cheng Chin Mong (1919–1999) and Marie Cheng Mui Kiang (née Goh) (1921–2003). Interviewed by Marc Rerceretnam on 22 January 1997. Personal collection; Catholics in Singapore (Unofficial guide). Facebook page, accessed 26 September 2019. Courtesy Alex Yam.

26 Anonymous. Church of St Teresa. (1954). In *St Teresa's Souvenir, Jubilee Issue*. Singapore: October 1954. p. 28; John Lee Khia Soon Descendants 李加顺 (December 1855–7 July 1927). Facebook page. Courtesy administrator Joseph Lee.

27 Anonymous. (1954). *St Teresa's Souvenir*, Jubilee Issue. p. 26.

28 Anonymous. (1954). *St Teresa's Souvenir*, Jubilee Issue. pp. 25, 28.

29 Interview with Philip Wee Peng Leng (1904–1991). Interviewed by Marjorie and Phyllis Wee, 18 August 1981. Personal collection.

30 Good Shepherd Church. Liber Matrimoniorum 1833–1857, SING 0001, #3, National Archives of Singapore.

31 Interview with Philip Wee Peng Leng (1904–1991). Interviewed by Marjorie and Phyllis Wee,18 August 1981. Personal collection.

[32] Anonymous. (1954). *St Teresa's Souvenir, Jubilee Issue*; Church of St Teresa. Or Imbrem Rosarum Nobis Infunde. (1947). In *St Teresa's Souvenir*, October 1947. Singapore: CYMA Church of St Teresa. (Page numbers unknown).

[33] Interview with Philip Wee Peng Leng (1904-1991). Interviewed by Marjorie and Phyllis Wee, 18 August 1981. Personal collection; Interview with Teresa Goh Mui Imm (1913–1995) and Marie Cheng Mui Kiang (née Goh) (1921–2003). Interviewed by Marc Rerceretnam, May 1988. The Goh sisters were aware of large consignments of rice, donated by the Wees (their in-laws) to the CHIJ Convent (Victoria Street) when they sheltered there for a few months in mid- to late 1943.

Chapter 5

# The Role of Women, Marriage and Matchmaking

*Before my breasts were grown,*
*I learnt that women in this world were nothing in this world that men have made.*
*Except in the role that men demand of her.*
*Your life is meaningless. You have no value.*
*Except as for a wife and mother. And be the very devil of a wife and mother.*
*Yes, look after your wife and family. Do everything for them.*
*Wrap them, bind them in the web of your providing.*
*Till they can't lift a finger to help themselves.*
*So that, husband, son and sister-in-law, they will all depend on you.*
*So that you control them and keep them in the palm of your hand.*
*So that the whole world knows your worth.*

Stella Kon, *Emily of Emerald Hill*<br>Constellation Books, 1989.

The nineteenth and much of the twentieth century was essentially a conservative time in Singapore. The rules and conventions in colonial Singapore were conservative; nonetheless people did occasionally break them. Basic rights such as equality in the law and protection against injustice hardly existed. Disparities between rich and poor were extreme, there were limited job opportunities around, and detention without trial was a weapon used by the colonial government to keep public opinion in line with their own interests. Singapore's various Asian communities in turn generally accepted social inequality as a *fait accompli*, especially in relation to their British masters. Ethnic divisions and other rivalries did exist prior to new immigrants' arrival in Singapore, especially so between Chinese clan groups, but the violence associated with this had begun to dissipate by the 1870s and 1880s.[1] By the early twentieth century, the various resident communities were somewhat assimilated with, if not exactly partial to each other.[2] However, the 'divide and rule' policies of the ruling colonial government ensured differences were maintained, and in some cases accentuated them among different racial groups and sub-groups. These artificial divisions manifested themselves in many ways, including a gender gap.

Cross-racial and cross-lingual communities like that of the growing Roman Catholic church helped overcome regional and lingual differences. Conversion to Christianity helped divorce some of the old prejudices carried in from the mother country, including the gender gap. And to a limited extent, the church became a medium for cross-cultural exchange and helped foster new friendships and ideas within a larger globalising world.[3]

## Women

In this already skewed environment, a woman's rights were even more curtailed than others. Basic laws that could improve women's lives were non-existent, such as divorce and separation rights, women's rights in marriage, or even protection of the family. The concept of women's rights was a luxury largely afforded only to the wealthy. Lengthy legal battles were expensive. Civil litigations, the serving of writs of summons to individuals living in what was still a largely mobile and transient society, was a difficult, protracted and therefore expensive process. To seek justice for lost property, rights to an inheritance, or legal recognition as a wife, was a privilege reserved for propertied and wealthy individuals.[4]

Society's expectations of women then were very confining as compared with today's modern standards. Early Singapore was a male-dominated society. Irrespective of cultural or racial background, most communities were patriarchal in nature and structure. In daily life, women played a secondary role within their families, often in the shadow of their fathers, brothers, husbands, sons, or other male relatives. Patriarchal traditions, reinforced by British colonialism, tied familial expectations of women to unpaid domestic responsibilities, marriage, and child-care. Matters such as education, property and wage-earning were a male responsibility.

The ratio of women to men in Singapore, or for that matter in the whole Malayan archipelago, was also extremely skewed in the nineteenth century. Due to heavy population increases because of the influx of male migrants from overseas, men predominated. Sending women to a chaotic 'frontier' town like Singapore was unheard of: no well-intentioned family would allow their daughter to be sent to Singapore without proper social networks to welcome and take care of her on the other side. In 1823 the ratio of women to men was 1:8. By 1850 the balance had tipped even more towards males: the ratio by then was 1:12, and in 1860, 1:15. The gender imbalance would only level off decades later, in the 1930s. The only communities with a better balanced gender ratio inevitably were found among longstanding local-born groups like the various Malay, Chinese, Indian or Melaka Peranakan communities. Nevertheless, established Peranakan Chinese communities were unlikely to accept lowly China-born and newly arrived (*sinkeh*) men within their ranks. Exceptions were made if a man was already established, regarded as industrious, or possessing potential. This was rare.[5]

Before the 1850s, the few Chinese women who arrived did so under the protection of their families. If they did arrive independently or with the help of others, they may have arrived as sex workers. No hard statistics exist to date; however, historians have estimated that around 20% of all Chinese sex workers in Singapore and the Malay Archipelago had plied the same trade back in China.[6] The majority had been forced into this predicament, having been sold by their destitute parents (some with the impression that their child might get better opportunities abroad) or abandoned because of family breakups. Brothel owners preyed on the precarious position of these girls and women.

## The different roles of women

It can be a mistake to draw broad conclusions about the social makeup of a community. Individuals within that community may hold varying views on an issue. However, Singapore society in the nineteenth and early twentieth centuries, was undeniably patriarchal. Men dominated, and controlled capital and property. In turn, women were expected to cover the domestic realm, including household matters, child-bearing and child-care. This largely cultural trait nonetheless cut through racial lines to impact all local communities, whether Chinese, Indian, Malay, Melaka Portuguese, Eurasian, European or British.

However, there were variations to these rules, and some were apparent within the multiracial communities of the Catholic church. It seems no account of a Catholic woman's life in those days has survived till today. What little information can be garnered from descendants shows that women's responsibilities and power remained within the social realm of the home, mostly in the form of nurturing children and family ties. Many women also took on the role of matchmaker not only for their own children but also for those of other family members and even friends. More importantly, these women's social circles determined the social and genetic makeup of future generations.

Taking the Teochew community as an example, girls and women traditionally played a secondary role to boys and men. Due to the emphasis on primogeniture in Teochew culture, social, economic, and political power in the Teochew community passed down through the male line, not the female. However, the role of women in new 'frontier towns' like Singapore evolved to alter this tradition. Due to the imbalanced population ratio between women and men in Singapore during the nineteenth and early twentieth centuries, girls and women slowly became a precious social asset and this resulted in a realignment of how they were perceived and treated. According to the Low family, in the 1870s, the family patriarch relied on his new wife to take care of the accounts for a new mercantile business which they had set up in the early to mid-1870s. The China-born patriarch also treated his daughters unusually well. He had three sons and four daughters. This point was strongly emphasised by his granddaughters when they recounted this to the author over a century later. The patriarch even took his young daughters back with him to visit his family village of Swalek/Xianlecun, in Shantou, in the 1890s. While in China, he refused to allow family members to bind the feet of his twelve-year-old daughter, Veronica, when she begged him not to allow their village relatives to follow through with their intentions. She had witnessed a cousin of the same age go through foot-binding, crying in pain, and understandably had been terrified by this experience.[7] This man's daughters were well educated up to high-school level and married off at the age of about eighteen. On the patriarch's death in March 1911, his wealth was shared equally between his sons and daughters.

In another account, a young orphan girl from the CHIJ town convent married an enterprising China-born Teochew boy around 1909. Her husband eventually built up a large manufacturing business but died prematurely in 1943. As her family tells it, it was on his widow's insistence that both her daughters and sons were given equal shares of the resulting inheritance. Today she is regarded by her descendants as a 'feminist ahead of her time'.[8] She died in 1962.[9]

Other sources relate stories showing freedoms, not necessarily equated with those conservative times. In the 1920s, an independently well-to-do woman's marriage irrevocably broke down. Being Catholic, she was unable to divorce her estranged husband. She purchased her own apartment near Stamford Road, took on a lover, and had a child out of wedlock. Despite these unusual social circumstances, she remained welcome within her staunchly Catholic family. Fortunately for the boy, he was accepted into his biological father's family business.[10]

Other accounts appear to provide a massive contrast in attitudes to women, wives, and daughters. In one wealthy Teochew family, accounts abound of the Singapore-born patriarch's paternalistic attitude towards his daughters. Daughters were only allowed a limited education, barely enough to read and write properly. While the girls were largely left uneducated, the boys were often educated up to tertiary level, when possible. The patriarch would keep emphasising how his daughters had to rely on their husbands not their own family.

How a woman was treated within her family strongly impacted on the roles she would take on later in life. In the case of the Low family, one of the Low daughters took an active managerial role in her husband's successful mercantile business in Bangkok after their marriage in 1904. When a quick decision was made to permanently move back home to Singapore in 1931, the main responsibility of tying up the loose financial ends in Bangkok was left to her. During the Second World War, with most of the men in the family killed by the Japanese, it was this same woman, now the matriarch, who took control of the family and managed their social and financial affairs, even after their exile to rural Bahau (Negeri Sembilan state, Malaysia) at a Catholic settlement set up by the new Japanese Occupation government. She would hold on to this role well into her late eighties, until her death in 1976.[11]

A well-known stereotype which existed at the time (and persists today) was that of the strict and controlling Peranakan mother. Several accounts of strict Peranakan matriarchs emerged clearly during the research for this book:

> *It was well known in the Peranakan families, the matriarch is the one who rules the brood, you know. Not the father … they would be the ones who decide who you marry. When my grannie was alive, she was the matriarch. But after she died, we were more free.*
>
> Anonymous, 3 January 2020.

The Peranakan mother-in-law's authority was paramount on the domestic front:

> *Woe was the daughter-in-law. They (Peranakan mothers-in-law) were very strict. Even the way you cut the vegies; cannot be too thick, cannot be too thin. The way you cook. "Micro-managing" is the word … they were very, very fussy.*
>
> Anonymous, 3 January 2020.

While social conventions within most Chinese dialect and even Indian groups remained strongly socially conservative, there is evidence showing that Melaka Portuguese and Eurasian community-families were much less harsh:

> In Peranakan (families) ... the girl coming into the family accepted they would be bullied by their mother-in-law. In the Eurasian family, "don't you dare try to bully me". (If) the mother-in-law try to control the daughter-in-law, the daughter-in-law will fight back ... it is not tolerated. "I am now daughter-in-law. I am not subject to you. I have my own life. I respect you but leave me alone."

Anonymous, 3 January 2020.

## Marriage

In the nineteenth century women had few lifestyle options apart from marriage. Employment opportunities were almost non-existent. Once married, a woman became legally responsible for 'hearth and home'. Even wealthy women could not claim their property as their own. Once married, a husband controlled his wife's property, her earnings and any profits she made. The wife could not make a contract nor engage independently with a court of law without her husband's say-so and involvement. In the best-case scenario, some women used marriage as an opportunity to open their own businesses, supported by their husbands. Deviations from these social norms were frowned upon. With the limited roles allowed for women, their primary duty was to marry and bear children.[12]

Despite these restrictions, the average Singaporean bride could at least expect to be the only wife in a marriage. Only monogamous marriages were recognised by the Catholic church. Nevertheless, there is clear evidence early Catholic 'towkay' Pedro Tan Nong Keah co-habited with at least three Catholic women in the 1840s and 1850s. There is no clear record on how the clergy of the day felt about this, however their ambivalence does come through the church baptism registers. The priests were meticulous about recording if a child or person was legitimate or illegitimate. However, in Pedro Tan's case, Frs Beurel and others do not mention the illegitimate status of at least two children born in 1845 and

1848 to women who are clearly not married to him at the time. His first wife Joanna, whom he legally married in 1841, died in 1847. Pedro Tan did eventually settle into a permanent monogamous marriage with his third partner, Anna Lim Ah Keow, by 1855.[13]

New immigrants seeking a spouse had either to take time away from employment and travel back home — an expensive exercise — or find an appropriate and willing female partner locally. This second option was made more difficult by the low ratio of women to men. In these conservative times, the pressure to form socially 'respectable' and 'acceptable' heterosexual liaisons was overwhelming, and competition for prospective wives in Singapore was therefore extremely keen. A small minority of men were married, and they were mainly Melaka-born Peranakans. Most of them were generally well-to-do. In 1848, Seah Eu Chin estimated only 2,000 Chinese men in Singapore were married. However, for single members of the Catholic community, hope lay within the Catholic church.

*A marriage invitation card, 1902*

Source: Donated by Ivy Bohn, image used with permission from the donor and the Eurasian Heritage Gallery, Singapore

## Homosexuality

Matrimony then was a clear life-path which every woman and man was required to undertake, irrespective of their own desires or inclinations. Historians have observed how a heavy gender imbalance within these early communities in the nineteenth and early twentieth centuries, affected family life and often created 'unhealthy social effects', a veiled reference to homosexuality. Same-sex liaisons, let alone same-sex marriage, were not an option, and illegal if revealed, under both secular laws and religious beliefs.[14] Marriage for heterosexual males was difficult at best, but impossible for homosexuals. In most cases, sympathetic families simply allowed such family members to remain single. Stricter families took harsher steps, in some cases forcing them to marry against their will.

> *The husband don't want* (bride's name). (The couple) *did not agree with each other.* Then (the bride's) *husband got "pondan"* (homosexual) *also.*
>
> Anonymous, 22 January 2020.

In one case, a young boy and girl, both from wealthy families, were forced into matrimony against their will, in 1929.[15] The groom refused to consummate the marriage. To make matters worse, he continually beat his new bride, forcing her to flee their matrimonial home. She returned to her parents' home, desperate for help, only to be told by her father that she had to go back to her husband because she was not her parents' responsibility any more. She now belonged to the groom's family. The situation resolved itself after the husband left the marital home. Thankfully, the husband eventually left his wife. Because she was Catholic, divorce was not an option available to the girl and she never remarried. Independently wealthy, she found solace with her elder sisters and their families until her death in the early 2000s. She never formally divorced.[16]

## Female orphans, and males desperately seeking respectability

In the nineteenth century, there were only a handful of orphanages in Singapore. In 1888, the Po Leung Kuk (保良局) was set up by the colonial government's new Chinese Protectorate. The Methodist church ran a smaller venture by the early 1890s, but the Catholic church had started their orphanage several decades earlier, soon after 1854, with the establishment of CHIJ on Victoria Street. These establishments provided much needed social services in the fledgling colony. Poverty and destitution were relatively high, and with no corresponding government initiatives to curb or address the ensuing challenges, it was left to these non-government organisations to address the issue.[17]

In keeping with the prevailing ideas of domestic female responsibilities, the orphanages encouraged many of their young charges to get married once they turned fifteen. The male suitor was often a local church member, who, carrying a recommendation from his parish priest, would visit the convent orphanage to choose his wife, with the permission of the resident nuns. In this way, the orphanages provided opportunities for male–female contact and inevitably acted as a platform for marriages.

Many of these 'convent girls' were isolated in a number of ways. They had been either wilfully or reluctantly abandoned, orphaned, or in exceptional cases abducted and sold. One 1899 account tells of a recently widowed India-born mother leaving her young daughter at an orphanage, only to die four days later herself. In 1900, a small girl was left at a Taiping convent by her homeless mother, who died several months later. Another account tells of an illegitimate boy, brought to the convent by his mother, who died six months later. Two sisters were put into the Penang CHIJ convent orphanage on the death of their father in 1919, when their mother went to work as a 'baby *amah*' or servant, for a European family. The two girls were visited by their mother every month. Not all circumstances were negative, however. One account told of how a former Indian barber, having left his four children at an orphanage, promised to take them back when he was financially able to do so. However, there are mistaken perceptions in some circles which imply that these orphans came from undesirable backgrounds. This view is not altogether fair.

Some of them may have been forced into their predicament, due to poverty or social isolation. Some managed to escape or were saved by concerned individuals, well-meaning clergy, or even by police. Many of these orphans, regardless of their difficult backgrounds, went on to marry and raise good families.

A bachelor searching for a bride would only get access to the convent on the recommendation of his parish priest. Most of these bachelors varied in age, from their twenties to their middle-to-late thirties. It seems safe to assume approval would only be given to men from a stable background and possessing the means to support a wife and family. While many of these bachelors were often themselves socially isolated from their family and kin networks in their countries of origin, their position as men in a patriarchal colonial environment would squarely place them in a position of power over an isolated convent girl. However, simply to typecast these orphan girls as the underdog would be a mistake, since although they had little choice, these marriages brought them financial and personal security. Most of the men who were able to marry, did so because they had the financial means, and therefore the approval of their priest, to do so. The assumption from this is that the poorer men were not afforded this privilege, at least not in the decades immediately following the establishment of the church in the 1830s. This comes through clearly in the church registers. Most of the marriages were celebrated at the city-based Saints Peter & Paul's church, set in a district where most of the better-off families lived, whereas far fewer marriages took place at the rural St Joseph's Church in Bukit Timah.[18]

These orphan marriages were common among the Catholic community. Many men, alone and away from their social and familial networks, resorted to choosing a wife from the convent orphanage.

> *He was ushered into the parlour while Sister went to find the eligible brides-to-be. She returned, sat down beside him, and warned him to look well at the girls who were about to pass through the room. The door opened; a young Tamil entered, walked slowly and awkwardly across the room, going out by another door, a second followed – this time a pretty Eurasian – the third – a big, buxom Chinese, of pleasant, good-humoured appearance. While the march-past was taking place, the*

*prospective fiancé chatted quite unconcernedly with the Sister. However, he had not his eyes on his pocket, for, on being asked which was the lady of his choice, he promptly replied, The third girl will make the best wife – it is she I prefer". The fortunate orphan was sent for. She came in shyly, hanging her head. Then she raised her eyes for her admirer. The Sister said to her simply: "See this Chinese young man here. He wants to marry you; would you like him as a husband?" She replied timidly, "If the Reverend Mother wishes it". So that clinched the matter. The marriage took place shortly after and the happy pair came to visit the Convent. Reverend Mother gave the husband this parting piece of advice: "Love your wife – she is our child and if you are not kind to her, we shall take her back".*

Excerpt from *CHIJ Victoria Street, 1854–1983* (2003), p. 28.

Many good marriages resulted from these arranged nuptials. Second-wave Catholic church philanthropist Jacobe Low Kiok Chiang's first wife, Penang-born Sarah Tan Chan (c.1850–c.1883), was a Catholic from the CHIJ Victoria Street orphanage. Her late parents were originally from Penang. She married Low in August 1867 and the couple had three children. Sarah was instrumental in the setting up of the Kiam Hoa Heng business in Bangkok in the 1870s. She acted as the company bookkeeper/accountant and was able to read and write in English. Unfortunately, she died in childbirth while delivering their fourth child, in 1883. In another case, John Goh Ah Seng (1851-1916), the general manager of Buan Hoa Seng (established 1883), a sister company to the Kiam Hoa Heng enterprise, married Spanish-Indonesian mix, sixteen-year-old Anna Maria Blanco (1860–1911), also from the CHIJ Victoria Street orphanage, in October 1876. They had around five children and lived at both their Oxley Road residence in Singapore and their alternate home in Bangkok. In about 1909, Peter Lim Ah Pin (1890–1943), who became a vermicelli manufacturer and was popularly dubbed 'Singapore's Bee Hoon King' in the early twentieth century, married a seventeen-year-old Peranakan girl Florence Yeo (1887–1962), another orphan from the convent orphanage. They lived in the Upper Serangoon Road area, where two streets, Lim Ah Pin Road and Florence Road, are named after them.[19]

## Orphanages

Orphanages played a key role in early community development in Singapore. Firstly, they provided a much-needed social service not delivered by the colonial government – support for poor, sick and destitute children. They also proved a major source of marriageable partners for local Catholic men in the nineteenth and early twentieth centuries. It is unknown precisely when the first Catholic church orphanage was established, but there is some evidence that such institutions may already have been up and running after Father Jean-Marie Beurel set up his schools by the early to mid-1850s. In the following decades, the main responsibility of running orphanages fell on the sisters of St Maur, who ran the CHIJ on Victoria Street. They also set up similar convent schools and orphanages, chronologically sequenced, in Penang, Selangor, Kuala Lumpur, Melaka, Kedah, Johor, and Perak.

For example, the mission-school education system covered the needs of more than half of the school-going population in Singapore in 1919. By the early 1940s, this figure had jumped to 64%.[20] The finance for most of this public service came from the Catholic church. Successive colonial governments did provide small annual grants, but this was a drop in the ocean, compared to the actual operational costs of running these initiatives. In a similar way, the survival of these orphanages came down to the tenacity, resourcefulness and generosity of the clergy, their volunteers and own parishioners, in their efforts to ensure that these vital services continued.

The life of an orphan was not easy. Opportunities were limited. The orphan's best hope was to marry into a good family, failing which, to find employment as a domestic worker. In the orphanage, an orphan's time was dominated by domestic duties, with little external contact beyond the orphanage walls. In keeping with the authoritarian nature of colonial society, orphanages often took liberties in terms of 'sanitising' or protecting girls from their own 'inappropriate' backgrounds. The son of a former convent orphan told of how his mother and aunt, their only surviving parent having died, had all their accompanying documentation burnt in 1915. This unfortunately included valuable land title deeds.

The Taiping-based nuns responsible at the time explained that their drastic action was necessary to help prevent the possibility of the girls' reversion to Hinduism: they feared that if any living relative realised that the children owned valuable property, they might consider taking them back into the family fold and would consequently reconvert the children back to Hinduism. (This kind of action appeared to be common practice among orphanages across the region. Similar church-based orphanages operating in Western Australia at the time commonly operated a policy of cutting children off from their previous life, to make it 'easier for them to adjust'). Life in the orphanages was spartan. No personal possessions were allowed — even toothbrushes and underclothes had to be shared with other children. Discipline was severe and corporal punishment was common. An orphan's day began just before six in the morning, starting with compulsory attendance at prayers. This was followed by a combination of chores, school, and the Catholic service of Mass, lasting until a quarter to four in the afternoon. Then it was back to chores, and finally, bedtime. This regimen continued six days a week.[21] The children were not allowed outside the convent and the gates were locked at night. The orphans' environment was emotionally cold. Generally, many nuns treated the orphans in a terse manner and scarcely fraternised with them. An ex-orphan of the CHIJ Victoria Street orphanage in the 1930s who

*CHIJ boarders, 1910*

Source: *Sisters of the Convent of Holy Infant Jesus, C.H.I.J. Victoria Street, 1854–1983* (2003), p. 31

was interviewed for this book claimed that one nun, Sister St Clement, had shown affection to the children. Affection-starved as they were, these orphans understandably were fond of and emotionally dependent on her as a result.[22]

In the nineteenth and twentieth centuries, education was not a priority for orphans. An ex-CHIJ Victoria Street orphan from the 1930s said they were only spoken to in the Malay language and were mainly taught domestic duties.[23] In contrast, paying boarders were spoken to in English and could attend a full day of school. This point is verifiable from church archival records. The Singapore-based orphans among the nuns' charges were educated to varying degrees; a few female orphans could just barely sign their names, while most could not. This harsh environment was exacerbated by the heavy financial demands involved in the running of an orphanage: maintenance was difficult, especially for an organisation with no regular income stream. Orphanages felt the pressure from the growing demand on their services. They also ran boarding schools where boarders paid for the privilege of living at the school. This was usually a relatively expensive option, open mainly to the affluent; in effect, the paying boarders subsidised the costs of running the orphanage. Boarding schools were run at the girls-only CHIJ and also at the boys-only St Joseph's Institution across the road, although the boys' version was much smaller.

*The St Joseph's Institution Boarders, 14 July 1910*

*Left to right: Tan Keng Sam, Tan Goon Soen, Tan Kion Wat, Tjon Pek Gie, Tan Kiong Bian, and Tan Kion Djun*

Source: St Joseph's Institution archive

Orphanages also acted as hospitals for sick and unwanted children. The sheer number of sick and dying infants left to the care of convent nuns is revealed by the registers of local Christian cemeteries. A close look at burial records gives an interesting glimpse into this tragedy. For example, between 30 June and 5 July 1911, at least 40% (approximately two to four a day) of all burials at the prominent Bidadari cemetery in Singapore were of convent or orphanage children. These children ranged between the ages of one week and nine months. The high death rate should not automatically be viewed as suspicious: infant mortality was extremely high at the time. Generally, infant deaths in Singapore numbered around 348.5 per 1,000 births in 1901; 232.2 (1921); 191.3 (1931), and 142.6 (1940). Such numbers undoubtedly owed much to medical shortcomings at the time together with the lack of funding, and were exacerbated by prevailing religion-based nursing traditions. Many French missions placed a greater emphasis on theology than on simple pragmatic health care; religious objectives and the salvation of the soul were more important than the health of the body. The preparation of the sick for deliverance into the next world was of utmost concern. This situation was not enhanced by the Catholic church's fervent push for conversions. It was only towards the end of the nineteenth century that closer scrutiny of church statistics revealed that most baptisms were conducted on the dying. All incoming children and infants were baptised immediately, sometimes by a priest, otherwise by an authorised nun.[24]

*CHIJ orphan babies, 1934*

Source: *Sisters of the Convent of Holy Infant Jesus, C.H.I.J. Victoria Street, 1854–1983* (2003), p. 49

*CHIJ orphans having a meal, 1924*
Source: Sisters of the Convent of Holy Infant Jesus, C.H.I.J. Victoria Street, 1854–1983 (2003), p. 46

## Intermarriages

The tradition of miscegenation and marrying outside one's cultural group has a long history in the Southeast Asian region. What are now referred to as the Peranakan communities (Indian, Arab, Chinese, and Portuguese) were already making themselves apparent from the fifteenth century and by the eighteenth and nineteenth centuries, had achieved prominence in both the social and economic life of Singapore and the Malay Archipelago. The story of the various Peranakan communities is well documented in local folklore and many history books. While the exact origins of the various Peranakan communities are still shrouded in relative mystery, it is an accepted fact that Indian, and later, Chinese settlers were established in the Melaka Sultanate from as early as the 1400s.[25]

However, by the nineteenth century, and the establishment of a British trading post in Singapore from 1819, the Catholic church inadvertently played a key role in the foundation of Singapore's own mixed-race Peranakan bloodline. If Peranakans represent the culmination of procreation or intermarriage between the foreign-born and local-born persons, then this is an important new finding. A spate of early intermarriages between China-born Teochew males and local or regionally-born native females, starting from 1834 and continuing consistently over a twenty-five year period, has been uncovered. These marriages took place within the multiracial congregation of the then newly established Catholic church on Bras Basah Road. Most of these marriages took place between China-born Teochew males and recently arrived mixed Portuguese women from Melaka. These Teochew-Melaka Portuguese marriages were a strong feature of Catholic society, approximately between the years 1834 and 1858. During the earliest batch of marriages that took place between 1833 and 1843, just eight marriages involving China-born men were celebrated. Only one of these marriages involved an ethnic Chinese partner. By the mid-1840s, women from the Melaka Portuguese community still featured significantly in unions with China-born Teochew males. However, among this number must be included a few local-born Chinese women from Singapore, Riau, Lingga and the neighbouring region, besides a few Malays (possibly orphans), a Melakan Chinese (possibly Peranakan) woman, and an Indian girl from Bengal.

Over this twenty-four-year period, a total of 125 marriages were celebrated under the auspices of the French Mission of the Catholic church in Singapore. Of this number, forty-two instances or 33.6% of marriages between 1833 and 1858 involved mixed-race couples. Of these 125 marriages, twenty-five instances or 20% appeared to be first-generation Peranakan unions. This figure is significant, as no other multiracial entity is known to have existed within colonial Singapore at the time. While these mixed marriages in colonial Singapore were in themselves significant, the numbers reported were still low, especially when seen in relation to the overall size of the congregations, which as we have seen in Chapter 2, had reached estimated levels of 300–340 between 1833 and 1851. Between 1834 and 1846, there were only eight marriages, all within the China-born community. Little wonder then that Father Jean-Marie Beurel wrote in July 1847 that marriage among the resident Chinese 'rarely happens, at least in this island'.[26] So, what was so special about these original eight China-born men married between 1833 and 1843, to enable them to find wives within the local Peranakan, Melaka Portuguese, Malay or indigenous communities? What did these eight Chinese men have to offer the consenting families? Perhaps simply that they were fellow Catholics.

The marriages between the Teochews and Melaka Portuguese began to dissipate when the new Portuguese Mission controlled by St Joseph's Church was completed in 1853. A large portion of the Melaka Portuguese population moved to the new church, a few hundred metres from the French Mission's Good Shepherd Church (later Cathedral), which they had been part of since the early 1830s. A few Melaka Portuguese did stay on, but their community no longer dominated the Good Shepherd congregation after that. This move impacted greatly on cross-cultural marriages as well. There was strong animosity between the rival French and Portuguese missions. With the move to the new church, it was highly likely that the Portuguese Mission clergy discouraged their flock from fraternising with worshippers from the other church.

The 1850s and 1860s saw a slight increase in the number of women arriving in Singapore from around the region, and sometimes even from China. In this period, marriages with CHIJ convent orphans also begin to pick up. The convent orphanage was never race-specific. Orphanages took anyone who needed help, on the proviso they were already Catholic, or would immediately convert if not. Eligible young Catholic men began to look towards the orphanage as a good source for marriage material. It is interesting to note that some young men were adventurous enough to choose girls of a different ethnic background from themselves.

These interracial marriages are extremely difficult to spot from the sparse information provided in late nineteenth-century church records, making it difficult to determine the ethnicity of many orphan girls. Most were referred to only by their first (baptismal) name, and therefore became ethnically unidentifiable. This author however found several cases involving members of the China-born Teochew congregation of the Church of Saints Peter & Paul whose brides are identifiable as being of Eurasian, Indian and Melaka Portuguese descent.[27]

By the first half of the twentieth century, the differences among the different ethnic groups in the Catholic church were beginning to dissolve. Superficial racial and cultural differences such as differences in attire were gradually dropped — there was a new trend towards more western dress styles, particularly among males. The mission school system established by Father Beurel in 1852 had fostered a couple of generations of English language-educated and middle-class Catholics. This new system had inadvertently de-emphasised cultural lines by creating new commonalities of wealth, English language use and western cultural mores. The new parameters of the urban middle-classes were based on the use of the English language and recognition of occupational and economic status. Mixing across cultural and racial lines became relatively easier. It is interesting to note that within ethnic Indian-Catholic parishes, early interracial couples came exclusively from the urban middle-class, not from the poorer rubber-estate working class.[28]

Intermarriage involving Indian partners was apparent in Selangor and Kuala Lumpur, initially in the Melaka Portuguese community and, to a lesser extent, among the Chinese too (see footnote 111). By the late 1930s and especially after the Second World War, intermarriage between Indians and members of the numerically larger Chinese community began to overtake those with the smaller Melakan community. In Singapore, all recorded Catholic Indian (male) to Chinese (female) intermarriage took place after 1937,[29] with seven instances taking place over a ten-year-period. There were fourteen such marriages between Indians and Eurasians or Melaka Portuguese between 1908 and 1948. Intermarriage with Malays was limited but there were two marriages between Indians and converted Malays. The limited number of Indian-Malay marriages was probably due to the religious exclusivity of both Christianity and Islam, which discouraged intermarriage, unless one party converted to the other's faith.[30]

The relationship between the Indian community and the Melakan communities was on much more equal terms than it was with the Chinese. However, racial power structures were also in play here. Most of these marriages were with the Portuguese communities, otherwise derogatorily known as the 'Lower Sixers'. Although they referred to themselves as 'Portuguese', most were racially Malay in appearance, with varying degrees of admixture of Chinese, Indian, Portuguese, Dutch and possibly British blood. Even within these communities, there was a racial divide between the 'dark' and 'light' Eurasians. The 'darker' Melaka Portuguese ('Lower Sixers') were looked down upon by their lighter counterparts ('Upper Tens'), which was again in keeping with the existing racial hierarchies. It was therefore relatively uncommon to find persons of the lighter variety intermarrying with Indians, whereas a match between a darker Portuguese and an Indian was socially palatable. The ratio of males to females was also more equal between these two groups, with eight Eurasian females to six Indian males.[31] There appeared to be almost no intermarriage between Europeans and Chinese or Indians officiated by local Chinese or Indian parishes in the early twentieth century. If such unions did exist, they were usually between European males and Asian females, never vice versa. These unions were solemnised at European churches such as the Catholic Cathedral of the Good Shepherd.

## Intra-ethnic divisions

Contrary to the early intermarriage that occurred within the church beginning in 1834, by the late nineteenth century, clear intra-ethnic divisions had developed among the three main Catholic communities, the Chinese, Indians, Melaka Portuguese and Eurasians. By the late nineteenth and early twentieth centuries, there appeared to be little intermarriage among the various Chinese dialect groups; Teochew married Teochew, Hokkien married Hokkien, Cantonese married Cantonese, and Khek married Khek. There was no written rule to fix these practices and the clergy appeared to ignore them.

> *Dialect groups look down on each other. Hokkiens called Teochews "Swa Beh" (wild horse).*
>
> Interview with Marie Cheng Mui Kiang (née Goh) (1922–2003),
> 22 January 1997.

This was accentuated by the ongoing practice of separating parishes by language. Hence Saints Peter & Paul's church was deemed a Teochew church, the Sacred Heart church was Khek and Cantonese-speaking, and the Church of St Teresa was Hokkien-speaking. Outsiders from other language groups were not forbidden to attend these churches, but as one Tanjong Pagar-based Tamil family recalled, they were frowned upon by the parish priest and were often told to sit in the back pews of the

Hokkien-allocated St Teresa's church.³² This was common practice from the middle to late nineteenth century and ended several years after the Second World War.

Inter-dialect marriages were not a common occurrence, judging from archival records and interviews with pre-war parishioners, although that does not mean that none ever took place. Many dialect groups did not mix outside their own circle. This was also determined by the fact that many marriages were 'arranged', and such marriages in turn were strongly determined by people's own social circles within their dialect-specific churches.

> *Last time people were very hard-headed. Very hard. You are Teochew, you (only) learn Teochew catechism. You are Cantonese, you learn Cantonese catechism.*
>
> Anastasia Lim, 22 January 2020.

Dialect group rivalry waned somewhat in the decades leading up to the Second World War. But it lingered on into the early twentieth century, even though Teochew-based philanthropy had helped build Hokkien, Khek and Cantonese Catholic churches from as early as 1910. In contemporary times, these divisions still existed in the 1950s,³³ but much less so from the 1970s onwards.

There were also divisions within the Indian community. Most of that community originated from the South Indian states, and was largely of Tamil, Malayali, Telugu, or Ceylonese (Sri Lankan) stock. Archival records show that like their Chinese counterparts, the Indians experienced little intermarriage between these groups prior to the decades following the Second World War. Another area of difference related to the Indian caste system. According to some old parishioners from the Our Lady of Lourdes Tamil church (all Indian Catholics were expected to attend the Our Lady of Lourdes Church up to the 1950s.³⁴) caste divisions and practices were 'banned' within the Catholic church. Nonetheless, like their Chinese dialect counterparts, Indian caste groups tended to marry only within their own groups. After the Second World

War, these divisions began to soften a little, but few ventured too far outside their own caste.

> *The Eurasians had lots of enclaves, so mixing up of the races was a bit difficult. Like if you go to Katong, there were tons of Eurasians, right. Serangoon Road and Bencoolen Street (had) lots of Eurasians. So, between school and church, mixing with other races was a bit difficult.*
>
> Loretta Santa Maria, 16 January 2020.

Similar divisions existed within the Melaka Portuguese and Eurasian communities. Within the Catholic church, they were clearly divided into two distinct social groups. These differences were defined by class, wealth, occupation, education, and even appearance.

> *Those who were educated looked down on those who did not have an education.*
>
> Loretta Santa Maria, 16 January 2020.

In the nineteenth and early twentieth centuries, the English-literate upper class or 'Upper Tens' was seen as superior to the mostly illiterate poor 'Portuguese' (known as 'the Lower Sixes').[35]

> *An Upper Ten marrying a Lower Six, and the parents can tell the Upper Ten, "I disown you. I disown you because you married a Lower Six, and you will get nothing". And sometimes in that kind of situation, and if the party is going through a hard time, and if he feels, "Why should I stay here and suffer?", he will divorce her. And he will just go back to his home.*
>
> Vicky Rodrigues, 16 January 2020.

During this period, there appears to have been hardly any cross-over marriages between these two groups, a fact accentuated with the completion of the Portuguese Mission's St Joseph's church in 1853 and the subsequent migration of Melaka Portuguese to the new church. Divisions between these groups ameliorated in the decades after the Second World War.[36]

## Social conservatism and divisions

*Nobody asked questions. We learnt catechism by rote.*

Interview with Stephen Cheng Chin Mong (1919–1998), 22 January 1997.

The early church congregations from the 1830s onwards were culturally mixed. Persons of all races used the same buildings, attended the same services, celebrations, and events. However, with the construction of new structures, a well-intentioned attempt was made to specialise services for different racial and language groups. While this may have been a common-sense move at the time, it unintentionally set artificial limits to the parishioners' social circles. This process began in 1853 with the completion of the Portuguese Mission church, catering solely to the Melaka Portuguese. Many Melaka Portuguese left the multiracial Good Shepherd Church which they had attended since 1832. The next break came with the completion of the Saints Peter & Paul's church in 1870. All the Chinese and Indian parishioners moved to this new church in 1847, leaving the older Good Shepherd Church to Europeans and 'Upper Ten' Eurasians. In 1888 the Our Lady of Lourdes church was established for the Indians, and in 1910, the Sacred Heart church was completed for the Khek and Cantonese dialect groups. Finally, in 1929, the Church of St Teresa was allocated for the Hokkiens.

Unlike the 1830s, 1840s and 1850s, the intercultural circles of the average parishioner thus became much smaller by the late nineteenth and early twentieth centuries. However, there was growth in other areas, such as the education system, which remained culturally mixed. The Catholic schools, established from 1852 onwards, were extremely multiracial, but this benefited only the younger generation. The older generations were limited by their now segregated church affiliations. In addition to this, social structures under the colonial British in Singapore were becoming more racially and culturally segregated, and this accentuated a new segregationist mood in this period, further discouraging social interaction. In one case, a young ethnic Chinese girl who married a Melaka Portuguese boy found herself ostracised by her elderly mother-in-law:

*My mother-in-law did not like me very much. She wanted her son to marry her own kind. They had a sense of belonging. I am an outsider. I sort of intruded into their family.*

Freda Pereira, 16 January 2020.

In a similar vein, pre-war attitudes seemed to support segregated marriages, often delineated by race:

*I think for marriages, parents would prefer you marry your own kind, for one simple reason; the parents themselves would know each other. So, you can guide your (own) children by looking (knowing) their parents.*

Vicky Rodrigues, 16 January 2020.

### Gender interaction

As in most patriarchal societies, in early Singapore, men were deemed to be superior to women. At home and at church, women played a secondary role, often in the shadow of their priests, husbands, brothers, or sons. These old traditions, reinforced by colonialism, tied familial expectations of women to unpaid domestic responsibilities.

The heavy gender imbalance in Singapore remained prevalent for decades and was only resolved from the 1930s, over a century after the establishment in 1819 of this colonial outpost. Traditionally, colonial employers did not encourage female labour due to perceived shortcomings in female productivity. In addition, there were few unattached women, primarily because many traditional families would marry off their females while they were still in puberty. The protected position women and girls had in traditional society was an obstacle to migration. Women were not allowed outside of the confines of their family, or unaccompanied by their fathers, brothers, or husbands. The extended-family system prevalent at the time, although providing a strong degree of familial 'protection' and 'stability', did not allow many women the freedom to emigrate on their own. To encourage men to return to their homes overseas, families tended to make their wives and children stay behind, in the hope that this would discourage the men from staying away too long.[37]

A young girl's standing was paramount. It was key that she not 'tarnish the good name' of herself or her family. It was taboo to befriend a boy outside of one's familial circles or be seen to be too friendly with male strangers. The concept of a boyfriend-girlfriend relationship was unheard of. It was objectionable to even contemplate marrying a non-Catholic, let alone a Protestant.

> There was an intangible barrier. There was no mixing of sexes.
>
> Interview with Stephen Cheng Chin Mong (1919–1998), 22 January 1997.

Breaching any of these rules not only soiled the reputation of the girl involved, but also that of her siblings and family. This was especially prevalent within the various Chinese-dialect and Indian communities. Members of the Melaka Portuguese community were less harsh. Boy-girl 'dating' among them appeared to be a relatively common practice, only adopted by the Indian and Chinese communities in the decades following the end of the Second World War.

Sexual promiscuity, though common among all groups, nonetheless was totally unacceptable. Virginity was of paramount importance for unmarried women, but male promiscuity was hypocritically tolerated, although in no way encouraged.

## Interaction between priests and parishioners

Social structures within the church before the Second World War were more austere than they are today. While the congregation appeared to mix well superficially, there were clear social demarcations between rich, middle-class, and poor. These boundaries were seldom crossed, especially in formal contexts. Even contact with the parish priest was restricted, and his opinion was never questioned:

> No one sees the priest for advice. The priest is not to be disturbed. Nobody disturbs the priest. If he tells you it is black, it is black. White is white. Nobody asks questions, not like now.
>
> Interview with Stephen Cheng Chin Mong (1919–1998), 22 January 1997.

Similarly, the relationship between priest and laity was somewhat distant. Ultimately, it was the individual personality of the priest that determined the level of interaction with his parishioners. While there is evidence showing that local priests did mediate in highly personal parishioner scenarios, this was limited to only extreme cases.

A few pre-war priests were portrayed as strict and domineering. Occasionally some of these stricter priests would take attendance during the mandatory Sunday mass:

> *You don't see a young girl talk to a priest you know. Not like the young girls nowadays. They are very friendly. Last time, a priest was a man after God's heart, you don't talk to him (laughter). Unless you are dying, then only the priest will come to see you. Not like now ....*
>
> Interview with Marie Cheng Mui Kiang (née Goh) (1921–2003),
> 22 January 1997.

In one account, a particular priest would wait outside the front entrance of his Indian-community church to spot latecomers to Sunday mass, only to chide them if caught. If a person should miss a mass, the priest would personally question the family during one of his later home visits. The typical relationship between priest and parishioner in this early period was described by one parishioner as being, 'seen but not heard'. A priest was a formidable figure — not to be approached unless necessary. German priests, of which there were a handful before the Second World War in Malaya and Singapore, were especially notorious in this respect.[38]

## Matchmakers and marriages between family groups

Matchmaking was a standard *modus operandi*, especially within the various Chinese and Indian/South Asian dialect groups. Matchmakers did operate within the Melaka Portuguese and Eurasian community, but to a more limited extent. Within these community groups, direct contact between potential marriage partners was undesirable. First contact was therefore heavily stage-managed. Family members, friends, or even informal matchmakers played roles in this process. In many cases, this role was taken up by an older female (occasionally a male) relative of a marriageable person; she or he would initiate the process by suggesting a match-up with a family. The use of the term 'arranged', as in an 'arranged marriage', needs to be clarified. The idea of free social interaction between the sexes simply was not recognised under the social conventions of the day.

> *Anybody could be a matchmaker. Normally it is the elderly woman ... a relative... there was no professional, no. As long (as they were part of) the Catholic community, it was your aunty ... meet in private at the church or meet in the New World (amusement park) or somewhere, you bring them in, like that. That is all.*
>
> Interview with Stephen Cheng Chin Mong (1919–1998), 22 January 1997.

Within the Chinese and Indian communities, unmarried persons, especially girls, were heavily discouraged from fraternising with boys. The concept of 'falling in love' was not seen as an important ingredient for a good match. 'Love' was viewed as something that grew with time during the process of living together as husband and wife. Married relationships were based more on obligation than passion. Many marriages in the late nineteenth and early twentieth centuries took place largely within a small group of families and were often determined by class and status. It was not uncommon to find siblings from one family marrying siblings from another one. The matchmakers were key in these developments:

> *(A matchmaker) ... "I see you got young daughters. Hey, you want your daughter to get married? I know a man .... I know this family". They then go through a history of this family: "Oh, the Chia family! I know them very well! I know this uncle."*
>
> *That is why, I know they all intermarry.*
>
> Interview with Stephen Cheng Chin Mong (1919–1998), 22 January 1997.

Back in the 1830s when the Catholic church was still in its infancy, matches tended to be based more on mutual benefit than familial links, race, or culture. In the first twenty years, there were correspondingly more multiracial matches; however, in the latter half of the nineteenth century, and with the expansion of new community groups within the church, such interracial marriages began to decline. This decline was also inadvertently accelerated by the channelling of congregations into separate churches from 1853 onwards, according to their language or dialect groups. By the late nineteenth and early twentieth century, gender ratios between men and women were more balanced and the establishment of formal social and familial networks helped matchmakers find suitors within a closed network of families.[39] An example of a matchmade marriage from the early 1930s was described to this author. According to the interviewee, the young Teochew Catholic bride-to-be's offspring:

> .... (she) did not know of my father at all. She never met him in her life. She doesn't know a thing ... I imagine they met on their wedding night!
>
> Anonymous interview, 3 January 2020.

This point is reaffirmed by another interviewee who said the bride and groom were not allowed to meet:

> They don't meet .... They know nothing .... their parents decided .... they cannot object.
>
> Anastasia Lim, 22 January 2020.

The social circles of the matchmaker, who was usually a family member, often determined and impacted on the long-term blood relations between families. While race appeared to have little importance in the early days of the church, by the late nineteenth century, the formation of clear dialect and racial parameters inadvertently limited intercultural mixing at the church and at the marital level. A clear example of this can be seen in research used for this book by Singapore-based family historian Juliana Lim. The work largely concentrates on a series of seven Teochew families, mostly based at the Saints Peter & Paul's church. The marriages are tracked from the 1850s till the 1930s and the research appears to show marriages consistently occurring within a select group of Teochew families, in this case the Lee, Ngun, Koh, Chan, Chia, Low, Tan and Wee/Ng families. Because of the widespread use of family-related matchmakers and the closed nature of church dialect or language circles, more matches tended to be made within existing familial networks than outside them. Hence it was common for married members from one family to again arrange a new match with the same family that they had already married into. Marriages between blood relations were not allowed, while marriages between cousins were only allowed provided dispensation from a priest was forthcoming. In Teochew circles, it was common to find several siblings or relatives from one family marrying into the same other family at the same time. One of the identifiable matchmakers was an elder sister from the Tan family, Regina Wee (née Tan) Mui Lian (1875–1942), and even her younger brother Thomas Tan Koon Boon (1890–1936), seemed to take a hand in the matchmaking process too. However, not all matches were equal.[40] Even within the Melaka Portuguese and Eurasian communities, where 'dating' appeared to be generally accepted by at least the early twentieth century, there also existed a strong undercurrent of traditional matchmaking:

> In 1920, my mum was supposedly of marrying age … about seventeen or eighteen years of age, and the family was on the lookout for a prospective husband. Where else to look at, was to go to church. And to notice the young guys there. The "Man Sebo" ("young men" in the Kristang language), they used to say …. they would spot somebody. They will spot someone, and then they'll need to know who the parents are, and by talking to the congregation, they will soon find out who the parents are. But the parents of the girl will not approach, but get somebody else in the family, like an uncle, aunt, or cousin, who happens to know that family. They'd then approach them, and to say, you know, if you'd be interested, I've got this very nice young lady and we'd like her to get to know your son."
>
> Valerie Scully, 16 January 2020.

*Photo of Jacob Lim Joo Khim and Maria Tan Guek Kheng, on the day of their marriage at Saints Peter & Paul church, 10 September 1935.*

Source: Cyprian Lim

Within the Melaka Portuguese and Eurasian communities, an intended union would be confirmed by a formal letter to the intended bride's father:

> *You write a letter asking for her hand in marriage, okay. The boy's parents will write to the girl's parents. And then there will be a response ... "Yes, we agree to it". And then they will proceed and meet up, and arrangements will be made, according to affordability – who can afford what. Because if they have a ceremony, and because Eurasians like to party, so we must have a party. And who pays for what.*
>
> Valerie Scully, 16 January 2020.

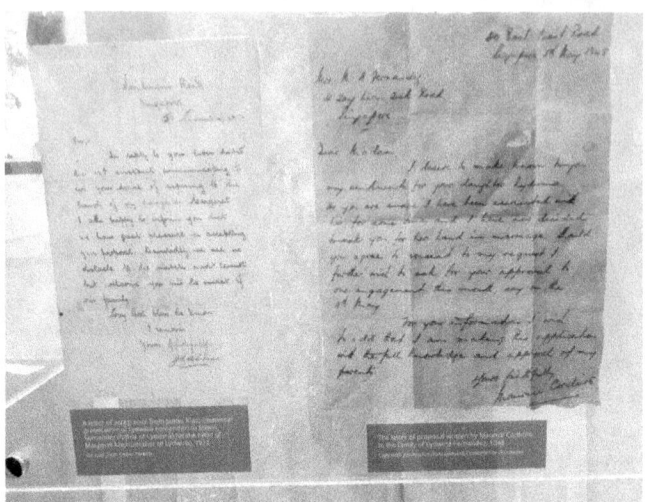

*Marriage proposal and acceptance letters c. 1912*

Source: Image used with permission from the donor and the Eurasian Heritage Gallery, Singapore

Several guidelines determined a match; knowledge of the family background, and whether they were good Catholics, their wealth and social status, played the largest role in the choices made. For some families, direct knowledge of the prospective marriage partner was not essential. Equal emphasis appeared to be placed on the suitability of the family, with the assumption that the intended spouse would probably be similarly suitable. Unfortunately, in some cases, this assumption was not always correct. In addition to being a matchmaker, Regina Wee (née Tan) Mui Lian (1875-1941) assumed the informal role of matriarch in her immediate family. This included her siblings, nephews, nieces, and cousins, sometimes several times removed. Regina was herself married to a wealthy military contractor and prominent church philanthropist, and she arranged for many relatives to take on jobs within the family construction firm as well as sometimes making affordable accommodation available to entire families.

*Photo of 21-year-old Mathilda Chia (1896-1985), in traditional Melaka-style Nyonya wedding dress on the day of her marriage to 23-year-old, Bangkok-based Joseph Low Kwang Seng at Saints Peter & Paul's church, 25 June 1917*

Source: Prrida Komolkiti, Bangkok

An account of a Catholic Peranakan wedding in 1904 was provided by the late Dr Peter Chia Teck Yam (1900–1989) in his unpublished memoirs, recalling what he saw as a three-year-old when attending the marriage of his unidentified older female cousin ('Twah Cheh'/Big sister) to groom Ng Ah Kow, probably at the Church of Saints Peter & Paul.[41]

*About the third year, when I had just* (unreadable) *go over with my pants* (unreadable), *there occurred a marriage between my cousin Twah Cheh and Ng Ah Kow, son of a wealthy farmer's widow. That event seemed to me the beginning of a conscious, though dim perception of my surroundings, people, and things. Impressions commenced to register in my budding memory. Twah Cheh was a tall, graceful girl dressed in Sarong and Kebaya and crowned with a beautiful kondai (thick, tall bun) of hair held in place by three larger gold pins. They were set with* (unreadable) *intans (diamonds). A three-rosette gold and diamond kerosang chain daintily held the sronal* (unreadable) *edges of the kebaya together. She wore a sarong of batik designs* (unreadable).

*She was shoed* (unreadable) *in a gorgeous pair of golden sandals that showed off her vermilion toenails.*

*I was Soy Koo* (unreadable), *the little page, which in Chinese tradition was usually filled in by a small boy who was a relative of the bride. I had to be appropriately accoutred. So, Mother fitted me with a suit of a red silk material that comprised a tiny jacket with knotted handmade buttons and a pair of trousers that had to be neatly folded in front before a small belt is worn. A skull cap made of a shining black velvet material with a silver* (unreadable) *was bought from a shop. The ensemble was completed with silk socks and a pair of scarlet red shoes.*

*Imagine how the little tot felt all gaily dressed up without mother to back him up. He had the duty to accompany the bride on a long travel* (unreadable) *to an unknown destination which was the house of the bridegroom. I had little recollection of the journey as I slept through it all. I was awakened by the bride Twah Cheh in her bridal chamber. There was Ng Ah Kow smiling at me. It appeared that I had slumbered soundly through a night on a couch. The sound of a Rongen* (ronggeng, a Malay dance tune) *filtered into the room. It was nearly noon time and the nuptial festival had begun. Twah Cheh bathed me and dressed me up in a hurry; then took me down two flights of steps to the ground floor where new mother-in-law and her daughter waited for me. There were many people, relatives, friends, and well-wishers of the Ng family, crowding the spacious hall. I was presented to each one and they all gave me Ang Pows* (lucky red envelopes) *tied with a loop of string that was placed around my neck! I was soon heavily loaded as the red packages contained silver coins. The ceremony terminated, to my relief, and I was taken upstairs, back to the care of the bride.*

Source: Dr Peter Chia Teck Yam. (1985).
*Memoir of a Straits Born Baba* (unpublished).[42]

## Marriage during the Japanese Occupation

With the advent of the Second World War and the ensuing social, economic and political mayhem, some Catholic communities took precautions to protect themselves. Within the Melaka Portuguese and Eurasian community, families with unmarried daughters were advised to marry them off immediately. In one case, young unmarried couples were advised by their parish priest not to postpone their weddings, due to the impending war:

> *The church (the parish priest at the Holy Family church, Katong) said "No, if the war continues for the next ten years, how are you going to, how is your relationship going to be if there is war …. you go home and tell your parents that I am coming to see you tomorrow" …. the next day, true to his word, he came and had a drink … "You will all get married as soon as possible, because if there is war and you have to run, then you run with your husband. If not, it is very difficult."*

Melanie Rodrigues, 16 January 2020.

In another case, some families appeared unwilling to have still unmarried daughters during wartime.

> *My mother and father, they were going out together … but then …. after the Japanese Occupation, their parents wanted them to get married, right. They did not want a single girl. They got married very fast, very simple. No hoo-ha, nothing. (Once a woman was married) she was a bit safer.*

Loretta Santa Maria, 16 January 2020.

The protection of young womenfolk was not the only reason for marriages at that time. In another case, a young Chinese Foochow man was desperate to avoid working for the Japanese army, in 1943. The Japanese army were forcing young unmarried males to clear jungle in the state of Negeri Sembilan. To many, this work was a death sentence. The young man needed to marry someone urgently:

> *I was in the convent* (in) *Bahau. He came to the convent to build a house ...* (and) *he saw me .... I tell you, why, because the Japanese want to open the land. So, if he* (worked for the Japanese army) *and open the land, he* (was) *sure to die. If you don't have a wife, you have to work. You go there, you no return. Sure die there. Because a lot of mosquito, you work hard, you got to cook for yourself, sure die. People all go there, no come back. Must have a wife, then no need to go.*
>
> Anastasia Lim, 22 January 2020.

A young sixteen-year-old girl lived under the charge of the relocated CHIJ convent school in Bahau (Negeri Sembilan), a settlement set aside for displaced Christian communities from Singapore. She was told by the nuns that a man wanted to marry her. As she did not oppose his proposal, they were married soon after. According to the interviewee, another girl married a friend of her new husband, probably for the same reason:

> *My mum married my father, because the following year, when the war broke out .... My grandfather announced to the children, those of you all who have got partners and who want to marry your partners, is best* (you do so) *... so when he announced that, my father allows me to marry anyone I wanted because of the war coming ... in fact in my mother's family, three weddings in three days. And all three at my father's house.*
>
> Vicky Rodrigues, 16 January 2020.

Despite minor changes between the 1830s and the 1940s, women's role remained secondary, overshadowed by the males in their lives, and destined to serve them. Society transited from a period in the 1800s where a skewed gender ratio had forced many men to sacrifice their hopes of married life and raising a family, to a brief period in the 1930s where married bliss was possible. But within a decade, war would bring a new meaning to marriage, with survival being its main driver.

In conclusion, while Singaporean society was very conservative and fearful of negative gossip, some segments of the Catholic community actively broke with convention. The rules inherited from old China, India, Malaya and even Europe were sometimes cast aside largely because these old rules just did not fit in their new environment. Many conservative rules were often broken by ordinary people. This may have been a simple but practical decision by new China-born arrivals to marry non-Chinese girls in the 1800s, when Chinese girls were not available. Many more well-to-do parishioners found wealth gave them opportunities to be independent and were therefore able to ignore otherwise damaging gossip. Some communities had more relaxed attitudes to issues of gender, such as the various Eurasian communities, with many 'dating' from the early 1900s. Likewise, domestic matriarchal rule was not tolerated, being something which was only adopted by other communities after the Second World War.

## Reference/Notes

[1] Kwa, C.G., & Kua, B.L. (2019). *A General History of the Chinese in Singapore.* Singapore: World Scientific Press. pp. 126–127.
[2] Rerceretnam, M. (2012). Intermarriage in colonial Malaya and Singapore: A case study of nineteenth- and early twentieth-century Roman Catholic and Methodist Asian communities. In the *Journal of Southeast Asian Studies*, Vol. 43, No. 2, June 2012. p. 305.
[3] Rerceretnam, M. (2020). Intermarriage, religious conversions, and new Peranakans within multi-ethnic communities in colonial Singapore: The development of early multi-ethnic Roman Catholic communities, c. 1830s to 1860. In *Chapters on Asia (2019)*. Singapore: National Library Board.
[4] Rerceretnam, M. (2011). *Black Europeans, the Indian Coolies and Empire: Colonialisation and Christianized Indians in colonial Malaya and Singapore, c. 1870s–c. 1950s.* Saarbrücken, Germany: VDM Verlag Dr Müller. pp. 330–332; Hassan, R. (1980). *Ethnicity, Culture and Fertility.* Singapore: Chopmen, 1980. p. 95.
[5] Rerceretnam, M. (2020) *Intermarriage, religious conversions and new Peranakans within multi-ethnic communities in colonial Singapore.*
[6] Tan B.H. (2003). Protecting women: Legislation and regulation of women's sexuality in colonial Malaya. In *Gender, Technology and Development*, Vol. 7, No. 1, 2003. pp. 1–30.
[7] Information from Clarice Wee-Thng (1950–), 22 January 2020.
[8] Information from Des Sim, 24 October 2019.
[9] Ho Ai Li, My grandmothers' road? Not many in Singapore. In *Straits Times*, 25 May 2017. https://www.straitstimes.com/singapore/my-grandmothers-road-not-many-in-singapore accessed 5 September 2019.
[10] Interview with Teresa Goh Mui Imm (1913–1995) and Marie Cheng Mui Kiang (née Goh) (1921–2003). Interviewed by Marc Rerceretnam, May 1988. Personal collection. Information from Clarice Wee-Thng (1950–), 22 January 2020.

11. Interview with Teresa Goh Mui Imm (1913–1995) and Marie Cheng Mui Kiang (née Goh) (1921–2003). Interviewed by Marc Rerceretnam, May 1988. Personal collection.
12. The legal rights of women were severely curtailed prior to the adoption of the 'Women's Charter' laws in 1961. For more information go to https://sso.agc.gov.sg/Act/WC1961 accessed 13 February 2020.
13. Information from Juliana Lim (1950–), 25 April 2021.
14. Rerceretnam, M. (2012). Intermarriage in colonial Malaya and Singapore. p. 318.
15. Interview with Michael Chia (1929–). Interviewed by Marc Rerceretnam, 21 January 2020.
16. Information on this source is confidential, upon request.
17. Rerceretnam, M. (2012). Intermarriage in colonial Malaya and Singapore. p. 311.
18. Rerceretnam, M. *Ibid.* p. 315.
19. Rerceretnam, M. (2020). *Intermarriage, religious conversions and new Peranakans within multi-ethnic communities in colonial Singapore*. Singapore: National Library Board (pending publication).
20. Rerceretnam, M. (2011). *Black Europeans, the Indian Coolies and Empire*. Saarbrücken, Germany: VDM Verlag Dr Müller. pp. 212–215.
21. Rerceretnam, M. (2012). Intermarriage in colonial Malaya and Singapore. pp. 311–313.
22. Interview with Anastasia Lim (b. 1927). Interviewed by Marc Rerceretnam, 22 January 2020.
23. Interview with Anastasia Lim (b. 1927). Interviewed by Marc Rerceretnam, 22 January 2020.
24. Rerceretnam, M. (2012). Intermarriage in colonial Malaya and Singapore. p. 314.
25. Rudolph, J. (1998). *Reconstructing Identities: A Social History of the Babas in Singapore*. Aldershot, UK: Ashgate. pp. 77–79
26. Brother Anthony (ed.). (1987). The Letter of Fr. J. M. Beurel relating to the establishment of St Joseph's Institution, Singapore. Singapore: St Joseph's Institution, 1987. (unpublished). p. 4. The relevant letter from Fr. J. M. Beurel to the Superior and Directors of the Seminary of Foreign Missions, is dated 4 July 1847.
27. Rerceretnam, M. (2020). *Intermarriage, religious conversions and new Peranakans within multi-ethnic communities in colonial Singapore*; Rerceretnam, M. (2012). Intermarriage in colonial Malaya and Singapore. pp. 318–319.
28. Rerceretnam, M. (2012). *Intermarriage in colonial Malaya and Singapore*. pp. 320–321.
29. Rerceretnam, M. *Ibid.* p. 321.
30. Rerceretnam M. *Ibid.* pp. 321–322.
31. Rerceretnam, M. *Ibid.* p. 322.
32. Interview with James Sebastian (1933–2020). Interviewed by Marc Rerceretnam, January 1999.
33. Mak Lau Fong. (1995). *The Dynamics of Chinese Dialect Groups in early Malaya*. Singapore: Singapore Society of Asian Studies. p. 5.
34. Rerceretnam, M. (2011). *Black Europeans, the Indian Coolies and Empire*. pp. 300–303.
35. Sarkissian, M. (2005). Being Portuguese in Malacca: The politics of folk culture in Malaysia. In *Etnográfica*, Vol. IX, No. 1, 2005. pp. 152–153.

36   Rerceretnam, M. (2020). *Intermarriage, religious conversions and new Peranakans within multi-ethnic communities in colonial Singapore.*
37   Rerceretnam, M. *Ibid.*
38   Rerceretnam, M. (2011). *Black Europeans, the Indian Coolies and Empire.* p. 306.
39   Rerceretnam, M. (2020). *Intermarriage, religious conversions and new Peranakans within multi-ethnic communities in colonial Singapore.*
40   For more information, see blog by Juliana Lim: *The Tans of Makepeace Road.* https://tansofmakepeaceroad.wordpress.com/
41   'Twah Cheh' may have been Lucian Kou/Khou Miong Tong (born c. 1890/1) who was a daughter of Marian Tan Zee Lian and Peter Kou Kuan Zou. Her groom was John Ng Ah Kou/Gou or Ng Tong Gou who was born in 1884. The wedding took place in 1908. Information from Juliana Lim, 13 July 2021.
42   Chia, T.Y., Dr Peter. (1985). *Memoir of a Straits Born Baba.* (Unpublished). Access to this document was made possible by Dr Chia's daughter Nora Chia.

Chapter 6

# Catholic Education Fills the Colonial Gap

After assuming control over the island of Singapore from February 1819, the British did little to provide essential services over the following decades. The education system was a case in point. The Singapore Institution college (later Raffles Institution) was established in 1823 via a board of trustees and funded by private capital. However, from its inception it was too small to cater to the needs of the entire population. Its original target group was the sons of local chiefs, and officers of the East India Company[1] but in later years it was largely patronised by the expatriate British and European communities, as well as the wealthy, and influential in general, and by the regional aristocracy. The colonial government did finance a Malay-language school system, but nothing else. Outside of this system, there was no standardised educational curriculum for the general populace. So derelict were the British colonials in this responsibility that in 1827 the Resident Councillor had the audacity to encourage local communities to set up their own schools.[2] Many responded to this call, and in 1832 MEP set up a 'boys' school'.[3] Like other similar unfunded, uncoordinated, and badly planned ventures, it was small in scale and somewhat makeshift. By this time, there were a handful of such uncoordinated schools, ranging from simple *kampong* set-ups to language-specific, and religion or clan-based ventures. Small-scale, with little room for future growth, these schools ran non-standard curricula. As a result, the vast majority of the young in Singapore were illiterate.

When the Roman Catholic church, under Father Jean-Marie Beurel, initiated a new push to create English-medium schools in the late 1840s, little did they know that this school system would become the bedrock on which the Singaporean education system would rely for the next century. By the first half of the twentieth century, the Singapore education system was dominated by three Christian mission school systems including the Catholic one. The other smaller systems were run by the Methodists and Anglicans. By 1919, there were 11,079 pupils enrolled in all schools in Singapore. Of this number, 1,216 attended St Joseph's Institution (SJI) alone.[4]

With the creation of formal Catholic schools in Singapore from 1852, all persons professing the Catholic faith had instant access to a high-quality educational system. This system continued the already established regime of mixing communities under one roof. Melaka Portuguese, Teochews, Kheks, Eurasians, Indians and some Europeans were educated together. The early numerical dominance of the Melaka Portuguese and Eurasian communities meant that they dominated the schools from their inception and well into the late nineteenth to early twentieth centuries. However, with the levelling out of the skewed gender ratio in Singapore (and the Malayan Archipelago) in the early twentieth century, bringing greater availability of females in the non-Melaka Portuguese communities, the enrolment of students from Chinese and Indian backgrounds grew correspondingly strongly.

When the Catholic church was established in Singapore in 1832 and new communities were converted to this new faith, not all fully realised that their conversion would later become a passport to a higher standard of living, from about 1852, when the formal Mission school system began to be established. Working men and women who were previously unable to read or write in the English language, soon found that their younger-generation family members were afforded the luxury of an English-language education, a prestigious asset thus far enjoyed by only a limited few in Singapore society. Membership of the Catholic community also provided a new step up the class ladder into the middle classes. A new generation of educated parishioners no longer had to follow in their illiterate parents' footsteps, doing backbreaking work on the docks or in plantation fields. Armed with a new education, many were now able to get much better paid white-collar jobs in professional firms or government offices.

## The founding of Catholic schools

With the completion of the long and often tedious task of fundraising and building the new Good Shepherd Church in June 1847, Father Jean-Marie Beurel set his sights on the establishment of a proper mission-based school and education system:

> One big thing is missing. I do not cease to think about it, nor to ruminate about it day and night. That is a Brothers' school. I have already spoken to you about it, and I shall speak about it again ....
>
> Letter from Fr Beurel to the Superior of the Seminary of
> the Foreign Missions, 7 December 1848.

Father Beurel was the primary driver of this initiative — he had been pushing the idea since 1846. His persistence gained him supporters as well as detractors within the Catholic church in Singapore. Within a year, he had formulated a clear plan to reach his target. He laid this out in a letter to his superior Bishop Albrand on 8 December 1847. He needed two or three teaching brothers, to be paid the equivalent of 400 francs annually:[5]

> .... without a school I can do nothing. In all there will be no stability.
>
> Letter from Fr Beurel to Fr Albrand, 8 December 1847.

For Father Beurel, a proper school system within the Catholic mission was imperative if the mission wished to continue working successfully in Singapore. He was fully aware that similar efforts by Protestant missions had failed before. However, he believed Catholic missionary efforts would be bolstered if coupled with a good school system.[6]

> It is the only way to lift them out of this mixture of heresy and schism which they imbibe either in their families, or in Protestant schools. God grant that I succeed in this undertaking which I place well above the construction of my new church.
>
> Letter from Fr Beurel to the Superior of the
> Seminary of the Foreign Missions, 4 July 1847.

From Father Beurel's assertion, it seems reasonable to assume that the only credible education then was available from 'Protestant schools'. He was most likely referring to the Singapore Institution (to be renamed Raffles Institution in 1868), which would have been controlled by British colonials of the Protestant faith. A few of Beurel's own younger, wealthier, and more promising parishioners may have been students there. Several small school initiatives were up and running at the time. A small girls-only school, St Margaret's School, was set up by the Protestant London Missionary Society in 1842, and the Protestant Raffles Girls' School a couple of years after.[7] Another small venture off the lower end of River Valley Road (now Zion Road) was run by the Protestant Rev. Keasberry, again from the London Missionary Society. The Catholic mission had commenced classes as early as 1832, and Father Anatole Manduit had started another school catering to farmers at his new rural parish in Kranji (later Bukit Panjang) in April 1847,[8] but these were small and uncoordinated initiatives. Father Beurel wanted something larger, permanent, and long-term.

*Father Jean-Marie Beurel (1813-1872)*

Source: *Chancery of the Roman Catholic Archdiocese of Singapore*

Father Beurel's concerns were correct, while leaving aside those focused on 'heresy and schism'.⁹ His vision of a quality, professionally taught, and standardised education system was essential for the younger generation and was as far-sighted as it was ambitious. By the 1840s, the economy in the region had changed irrevocably. European power structures had implanted themselves in Southeast Asia to the point where trade, business, communications, and political systems were all orientated towards Europe, and not to China or India, as had been the norm for more than a millennium. It was imperative to educate and ready the new local-born generation in the new *lingua franca* of business and power, the English language. It was also important to embed this system in a curriculum which could be recognised within a wider educational realm — enabling future graduates to venture into tertiary studies, usually overseas.

## St Joseph's Institution

On Sunday 6 June 1847, Father Beurel announced to his congregation that he wanted to establish new schools to be run by Christian brothers and nuns. He took St Joseph as the patron saint for this new undertaking, and formulated the following guidelines for this first new school:

- The school will be for boys only.
- The following subjects will be taught: English, French, Chinese and Malay languages, Mathematics, Bookkeeping and Drawing.
- The school will be open to everyone; it will accept both Catholics and non-Catholics.
- The school will not interfere in the faith of non-Catholic pupils. Religious instruction to be given only to Catholic boys, before or after school hours.¹⁰

Donations to the new school, SJI, were sought from both within and outside the Catholic community; Father Beurel was so enthused by the project that he used his own money to help realise it (by 1861 the school owed Beurel $2,977).¹¹ The school was formally opened on 1 May 1852, with three teachers. Prior to the completion of a purpose-made school building, the old Bras Basah Road chapel built in 1833 would be used temporarily. The school started off with a handful of students, some of whom were identified fifty years later, in 1902, as:

> .... Mr. John Schreeder, Mr. Martia, Buan Seng the shipping clerk of a large European firm, and Tan Hay Seng, the son of Pedro No Kia, a wealthy Chinese member of the congregation in the older days.
>
> Source: CB Buckley, *An Anecdotal History of Old Times in Singapore*, 1984 (1902), p. 270.

St Joseph's Institution c. 1900

Source: St Joseph's Institution archives

Within seven years, in 1860, there were 110 registered pupils enrolled in SJI. By 1885 enrolments had jumped to 225; 482 in 1893; 679 in 1905; 1,216 by 1919, and to a high of 1,586 in 1923. By the 1930s, there was a large growth in Catholic schools. Enrolments in SJI reduced slightly and levelled off to around 1,200 with the opening in 1933 of another boys' school, St Patrick's School in Katong.[12] In 1933, the St Nicholas Girls' School was established by the CHIJ (Victoria Street) as a primary school for girls and two years later, the Catholic High School (Sino-English Catholic School) for boys was founded by Catholic layperson Paul Lee and Rev Edward Becheras.[13] Both schools were run as Chinese language medium schools. In 1916 two schools, the Holy Innocents English and

Holy Innocents Chinese were set up by the parish of the Nativity church. In 1936, the Montfort Brothers of St Gabriel took over or began several educational initiatives of their own in the Aukang/Hougang area where there existed a large concentration of Teochew Catholics, since the 1850s.[14]

During the Japanese Occupation, SJI was run as the Bras Basah Boys' School but resumed as a mission school after the Japanese surrender in 1945.

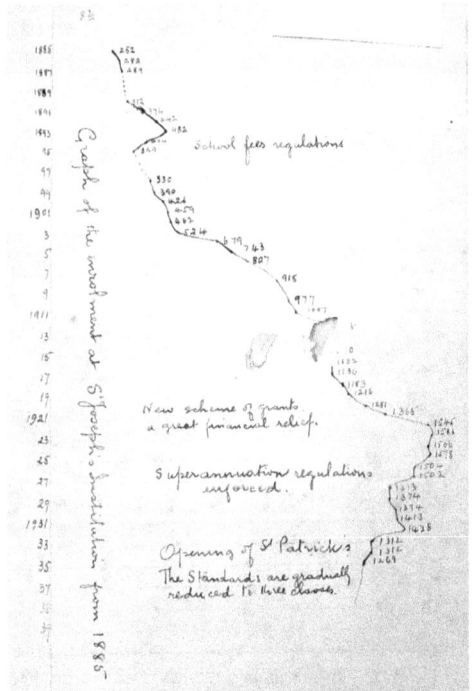

*Enrolment numbers at St. Joseph's Institution, 1885–1938*
Source: Diaries of Brothers, PD111-2, 1902–1946, SJI archives

## The Convent of the Holy Infant Jesus

In the early days of the Catholic community, a vast majority of Catholic women were illiterate. While the author was unable to access convent archives for research purposes, information collated from church marriage records provides an interesting insight. Most young women entering matrimony were clearly illiterate, especially in the 1830s–1850s.

Few could sign their names in the marriage registry book, many simply leaving an 'X' where their signature should be. To be fair, many men were also in this same predicament. However, this varied greatly. While most Teochew men were illiterate, a considerable number were not, and signed their names in legible Chinese script. The Melaka Portuguese were mostly illiterate, both men and women, while the educated portion of this community, the 'Upper Tens', was largely literate. A large proportion of early Tamil parishioners was able to provide signatures in the Tamil script. Persons of European or British background were always literate in the English language.[15]

*Convent of the Holy Infant Jesus, Victoria Street, early 20th century*

Source: *Sisters of the Convent of Holy Infant Jesus, C.H.I.J. Victoria Street, 1854–1983* (2003), p. 4

Several church groups did cater for female education, but these efforts were few and far between.[16] Traditional practices imposed on girls often had a detrimental effect on the educational opportunities of boys too: in 1905, a Methodist church paper reported how a number of their 'brightest young men' were often forced to leave school to find employment because of the dowry requirements of their unmarried sisters.[17] Such costs appeared to be among the biggest impediments to female education. Women, apart from being the 'most expensive item in the family', could not offer any return on the cost of an expensive education. In fact, female education was deemed a negative in the marriage stakes. Discriminatory stereotypes of educated women as being devoid of womanly grace and modesty, were common.[18]

With the successful establishment of SJI assured, Father Beurel next turned to the education and welfare of girls and young women. Once again, with Beurel's forthright and decisive guidance, the Convent of the Holy Infant Jesus (CHIJ) was set up within two years of SJI's opening, just across the road. After failing to get financial support from the colonial government, Beurel again used his own money to purchase property on Victoria Street for the purpose of establishing a convent. He personally sought assistance from the French order, the Sisters of St Maur.

By February 1854 the sisters had arrived in Singapore, prepared to take over the project. They immediately set up an orphanage in 1854, started a boarding school for paying students and began classes soon after their arrival; by 1855 they were already overseeing the building of a new school. Predictably, the convent had a different aim from the boys' schools, including being devoted to far more than education alone. While it concentrated on the education of young women, girls, and to a limited extent young boys too, CHIJ also fulfilled a key social welfare function, a role much needed by the young colony. The sisters provided the medical services so far ignored by the British colonial government, as well as shelter and protection to destitute young women and children. Up to that point, Singapore was then still a 'frontier' town, its population comprising primarily new and mostly male arrivals. Apart from the indigenous Malay or local resident communities, the rest of the population did not have a social or familial network to fall back on. This environment had created a large community of destitute poor and of children at serious risk. Many had been abandoned, or even privately incarcerated, largely because of poverty or the death of their parents, family, or caregivers.[19]

The need to educate young women was not felt strongly in the Singapore of the 1850s, neither among the various Chinese dialect groups, nor among most other communities. Consequently, the educational side of CHIJ did not grow and develop as fast as it did at

SJI boys' school across the road. Forty years after its foundation, in 1894, the convent school had only 167 students, while the boys-only SJI had more than 400 students.[20] Perceptions of the role of girls and young women were changing fast, even among the socially conservative Asian communities. By 1900, the number of CHIJ students had almost doubled to more than 300 pupils, and by 1904 the school had formed a Junior Cambridge (exam) class (sixteen-year-olds). A mere four years previously, no female even aspired to this educational level.[21]

## The key role played by Catholic schools

The British colonial education system was replicated across Singapore and the Malayan Archipelago. It was grossly inadequate and piecemeal. In 1923, the Inspector of Schools (Singapore and Labuan) admitted there were 'too many children in the schools, they are overcrowded and working under adverse conditions.'[22] This was despite the fact that English-medium education had been instituted in the Malayan Archipelago as early as 1816 in Penang and 1823 in Singapore. By the end of the nineteenth century, there were about 9,000 students in English-language schools located in Singapore and the Malayan Archipelago. Most of them catered only for the lower levels, with little opportunity for upper secondary and none for tertiary learning. Teacher-training was non-existent until 1907 and a trade-related technical school[23] opened only in 1906. The latter did not attain college status until just before the Japanese Occupation in 1942. A medical school and an arts college were set up in 1904 and 1920 respectively, with the primary purpose of training 'assistants'. There was no university until well after 1945.[24]

With the colonial government largely ignoring the educational needs of the people it governed, missionary bodies found it necessary to start up a series of schools funded by private organisations and philanthropists. By the 1860s, government implemented a grant-in-aid system, which provided small annual grants to recognised schools. However, even with this financial assistance, much of the education system was heavily reliant on missionary bodies, private organisations and the goodwill of philanthropists. In 1863, SJI began charging school fees to cover costs;

that same year, the school was officially recognised by the colonial government and began to receive a small grant.

## Colonials keeping 'natives' in their place

Why were the British colonials so reluctant to invest in their colonial charges? According to an April 1936 'Memorandum on Education Policy in the Straits Settlements and in the Federated Malay States', British officialdom stated they preferred to concentrate on the proliferation of minor dialect-specific schools, not English-medium ones, to 'avoid any challenge to colonial rule'. It also noted that an unemployable native could 'become dissatisfied and, far from being an asset, is a danger to the community in that his outlook becomes warped and bitter.'[25]

> *An English education will turn the peasant into an urban-minded "gentleman" and will increase the concentration of population in the towns. It is said that English education would not be provided in the rural areas. Perhaps not. But since, as has been stated above, a knowledge of English is necessary for the best jobs and since the rural inhabitant will see (as indeed he sees already) all the plums going to boys with English education, will he rest content in his village? Will he not clamour for an English education too? Certainly he will. Therefore let us restrict English education as much as possible and remove the temptation from the peasant.*
>
> Source: A Memorandum on Education Policy in the Straits Settlements and in the Federated Malay States, April 1936, Public Records Office, SSOC (misc.), p. 39.

Financial assistance to English-medium schools was only encouraged on the proviso that it was in line with the needs of government and industry, and even then, it was meagre indeed. For example, between the years of 1875 and 1900, the colonial government allocated less than 1% of gross national product to the education system in the Straits Settlements.

## References/Notes

1. Prasad, J.M Vina, & Koh, J. Raffles Institution. In *Infopedia*. Singapore: National Library Board. https://eresources.nlb.gov.sg/infopedia/articles/SIP_17_2004-12-21.html accessed 10 February 2020.
2. Song, O.S. (1923/2016). *100 Years' History of the Chinese in Singapore*. pp. 36–37.
3. Buckley, C.B. (1902/1984). *An Anecdotal History of Old Times in Singapore*. p. 247. There is no evidence a proper school based on a sound education curriculum was established in 1832. However, in 1840, a decision to push ahead with a new church was set in place, and the old Bras Basah Road chapel was to be used as a permanent school.
4. Rerceretnam, M. (2011). *Black Europeans, the Indian Coolies and Empire: Colonialisation and Christianized Indians in colonial Malaya and Singapore, c. 1870s–c. 1950s*. Saarbrücken, Germany: VDM Verlag Dr Müller. pp. 218–219.
5. Beurel, J.M. *The Letters of Fr J. M. Beurel relating to the establishment of St. Joseph's Institution Singapore*. Translated, Edited, and with a Monograph by Rev. Brother Anthony, St. Xavier's Institution, Penang. (Unpublished). St Joseph's Institution Archives. p. 2.
6. J. M. Beurel, *Ibid*. p. 4.
7. Prasad, J.M. Vina, & Koh, J. Raffles Institution. In *Infopedia*.
8. Buckley, C.B. (1902/1984). *An Anecdotal History of Old Times in Singapore*. p. 251.
9. Beurel, J.M. *The Letters of Fr J. M. Beurel relating to the establishment of St. Joseph's Institution Singapore*. p 6.
10. Buckley, C.B. (1902/1984). *An Anecdotal History of Old Times in Singapore*. p. 261.
11. Buckley, *Ibid*. pp. 263–264.
12. SJI Brother's Diary, 1902–1946. Singapore: St. Joseph's Institution. PD111-2. (Unpublished). p. 82.
13. Lim, C. (2019). *My Maternal Roots: A Story of Family, Faith and Freedom*. Singapore: World Scientific Press. pp. 176-179.
14. Seah, S. (2020). *My Father's Kampung: A History of Aukang and Punggol*. Singapore: World Scientific, pp. 17–35.
15. Good Shepherd Church. Liber Matrimoniorum 1833–1857. Singapore. The issue of literacy would have improved over the decades, following the opening of mission schools from 1852.
16. Anonymous. The Anglo Tamil School, Singapore. In *The Malaysia Message*, Vol. XV, No. 3, December 1905, p. 25.
17. Anonymous. Tamil Wedding Dowries. In *The Malaysia Message*, Vol. XV, No. 1, October 1905. p. 2. This was supposedly common among both Hindu and Christian boys. These costs may not relate specifically to dowry payments but could involve general marriage expenses. For example, the family of local Eurasian brides were often responsible for the costs of the expensive wedding party following a wedding. Many families took on loans to cover these costs. (Interview with Valerie Scully, 16 January 2020).

18 Davies, Mrs E.V., M.A. Women's Education in South India. In *The Malaysia Message*, Vol. 37, No. 4, January 1927. p. 6; Anonymous. Our Women's Corner. In The Indian, 28 March 1936, Kuala Lumpur. p. 15.
19 Buckley, *An Anecdotal History of Old Times in Singapore*', p. 253–255.
20 SJI Brother's Diary. (1902–1946). p. 82; Anonymous. Convent of the Holy Infant Jesus. (1983/2003). *C.H.I.J. Victoria Street 1854–1983* (Singapore: CHIJ/NLB). p. 15.
21 Buckley, C.B. (1902/1984). *An Anecdotal History of Old Times in Singapore*. p. 268; Anonymous. C.H.I.J. Victoria Street 1854–1983. p. 19.
22 Mangan, J.A. (ed.). (1993). *The Imperial Curriculum: Racial images and education in the British colonial experience*. London: Routledge. p. 154; Puthucheary, M. (1993). Indians in the Public Sector in Malaysia. In *Indian Communities in Southeast Asia*. Singapore: Institute of Southeast Asian Studies, 1993. p. 337; *Proceedings and Report of the Committee appointed to consider the problem of destitution among the various Sections of the Community*, Singapore. (1923). p. 34.
23 *Ibid*. (1923). p. 35. In these Proceedings, the Inspector of Schools (Singapore and Labuan), H. T. Clark, admitted that there was no provision for proper trade-related education in 1923.
24 Singh, K.S. (1969). *Indians in Malaya: Immigration and Settlement 1789–1957*. Cambridge: Cambridge University Press. p. 68.
25 'A Memorandum on Education Policy in the Straits Settlements and in the Federated Malay States', April 1936, Public Records Office, (misc.), p. 39; Mangan, J.A. (ed.). (1993) *The Imperial Curriculum: Racial images and education in the British colonial experience*. p. 164.

Chapter 7

# The Roman Catholic Church: Architect of Multiracial Education & Social Services in Colonial Singapore

Historically, the Roman Catholic church in Singapore (and in the Malayan Archipelago) has played a seminal role in the development of modern society. Emissaries of the faith arrived on the island in 1821 with the idea of setting up a base there. A decade later, a permanent base was established on Bras Basah Road. While the primary aim of the French Roman Catholic mission was religious outreach, over the next century it did much more. Apart from spreading its spiritual and evangelical message, the mission inadvertently also became the backbone of key community development initiatives in Singapore.

The 144 years (1819–1963) of British colonial rule in Singapore largely constituted a government-sanctioned, profit-making exercise for developing and growing British trade and profit. Throughout the era of the British Empire, the colonials created captive markets for British-made goods, repatriating the profits back to Britain. Singapore was no exception, and the colonial government furthermore ignored the essential responsibilities of government, such as the education and social welfare of the population. These responsibilities were instead taken on by faith, charity, and clan-based community organisations. If social or physical infrastructure was developed, it was primarily for the benefit of British interests, not those of the local population. The so-called British legacy — of education, of the English language, and community development — has been greatly exaggerated.

The social welfare ventures set up by the Catholic church organisations were run with little colonial government assistance (generally small annual grants), benefiting rather from the philanthropic endeavours of these organisations themselves. Within the Catholic church, an active philanthropic business network developed from the 1840s, coming into its own in the 1880s. In other words, institutions like the Catholic church assumed what should have been the role of the colonial government, and almost single-handedly propped up essential services in Singapore for over a century.

## Multiracialism

The Catholic church also inadvertently promoted multiracialism in Singapore, a concept which would gain prominence only after independence from the British was achieved in the 1960s. The Southeast Asian region has its own long history of multiracialism, especially in relation to its old Peranakan communities. Traders from China, India, the Middle East and even Europe,[1] spawned hybrid communities which became part and parcel of the local and regional landscape. After the arrival of the British colonials in 1819, and their attempts to compartmentalise and separate communities into different parts of the island, the early Catholic church accidentally countered these negative moves by providing opportunities for the culturally diverse church community to mix in a fair and harmonious social environment. Differences did exist within these communities; however, these often related more to class snobbery than to racism.

While this exercise in multiracialism reaped impressive results in the first two decades of the church's existence, the beneficial effects dwindled once the church began to expand. The practice of separating congregations by language group unintentionally divided communities. Apart from employment or school, opportunities for socialising gradually narrowed to mixing with 'your own kind' over weekends. The limiting of social circles in turn influenced matchmakers and their choices of partners for their clients, impacting on interracial marriages. This unfortunate outcome did not mend itself till well after the Second World War, when social barriers began to fall, and cross-dialect marriages became the norm among the Chinese. In the Melaka

Portuguese community, it became more common for so-called 'Upper Tens' and 'Lower Sixes' to mix and intermarry. Among the different Indian communities, cross-caste marriages were beginning to take hold. Educational level, occupation and class status became stronger factors in decisions on marriages and friendships. Interracial marriages gained popularity in the coming decades, but the idea still never rekindled the fervour of the early years of the Catholic church.

## Education

Father Jean-Marie Beurel's idea of establishing a comprehensive English-medium school in the 1840s became the backbone of the Singapore school system, and would dominate the colonial educational system for a century. While this created an automatic educational pathway for Catholic communities in Singapore, Catholic schools clearly did not exclude those not of the same faith. This generosity granted many non-Catholics an opportunity to attain a proper education and contributed towards the building of a new multiracial and multifaith middle class.

St Joseph's Institution was the first all-boys' school to be opened, in 1852, and within two years was followed by the mainly girls' school, the Convent of the Holy Infant Jesus (CHIJ). For the Catholic community, this helped close the deep social divisions that had existed in the early days of the church. From the 1850s onwards, all Catholics were offered similar educational opportunities. For many families, learning to read and write for the first time acted as a passport out of low-paid menial employment and into better-paid professional jobs. The massive divisions between the 'haves' and 'have-nots' were considerably reduced.

## Social services

Inadequate social services were a pressing issue in nineteenth-century Singapore, and one which was not properly addressed by the British colonial government. Destitution, poverty, child abandonment, the lack of health services, and prostitution were all major problems. With the foundation of the CHIJ in February 1854, Reverend Mother St Mathilde and three fellow nuns started up an orphanage and a boarding school and began teaching classes.[2] The orphanage also acted as a hospital for sick and unwanted children.[3] Nursing expertise acquired from their work made the nuns an indispensable resource when the first government hospital was set up in Singapore in the 1880s, six decades after the founding of British colonial Singapore.[4]

The Catholic church and its institutions played a seminal role in the development of modern Singapore, a role not fully recognised in current histories. Ironically, it was British imperialism that favoured the genesis of such religious ventures in colonies like Singapore. While British imperialism was profit-driven, aimed at enriching British interests and government coffers, the primary objective of most religious orders was the proselytising and expansion of their faith among non-believers. However, the church's role as an early incubator of multiracialism, English-language public education and essential social services was an unforeseen outcome of its original declared intentions. Largely due to the selfishness of the British colonial project, the Roman Catholic church and its institutions powered the development of a modern community in Singapore.

## References/Notes

[1] Trocki, C.A. (1990). *Opium and Empire: Chinese Society in Colonial Singapore, 1800–1910*. New York: Cornell University Press. p. 5.

[2] Buckley, C.B. (1902/1984). *An Anecdotal History of Old Times in Singapore*, pp. 253–254; Anonymous, C.H.I.J. 1854–1983. p. 18.

[3] Rerceretnam, M. (2012). Intermarriage in colonial Malaya and Singapore: A case study of nineteenth- and early twentieth-century Roman Catholic and Methodist Asian communities. In *Journal of Southeast Asian Studies*, Vol. 43, No. 2, June 2012. pp. 313–314.

[4] Lee, Y.K. The origins of nursing in Singapore. In *Singapore Medical Journal*, Vol. 26, No. 1, pp. 54–55.

www.ingramcontent.com/pod-product-compliance
Lightning Source LLC
Chambersburg PA
CBHW072006290426
44109CB00018B/2147